HOPE THIS HELPS

BENJY KUSI

HOPE THIS HELPS

How to be Kinder to Yourself and Others

HEADLINE

First published in 2023 by
HEADLINE PUBLISHING GROUP

1

Cataloguing in Publication Data is available from the British Library

Hardback ISBN 978 1 0354 0120 8

Typeset in Berling by CC Book Production

Printed and bound in Great Britain by Clays Ltd, Elcograf S.p.A.

HEADLINE PUBLISHING GROUP
An Hachette UK Company
Carmelite House
50 Victoria Embankment
London EC4Y 0DZ

www.headline.co.uk
www.hachette.co.uk

For anyone who has ever dreamed of better
and wanted more for themselves and the world.

CONTENTS

Introduction 1

1. Why should we be kind? 3

2. Why it's not selfish to choose yourself 17

3. Why it's OK to change your opinion
   as you learn 31

4. Why you shouldn't care what others think 47

5. Why impact means more than intent 61

6. Why it's important to understand our privilege 71

7. How we can be better to each other 87

8. Why intersectionality and our
   uniqueness is important 105

9. Why equity is better than equality   121

10. Why we shouldn't 'other',
    objectify or stereotype people   135

11. How to apologise   151

12. Why we should listen to others
    and be empathetic   167

13. Why we should respect how people
    want to be addressed   181

14. Why we should uplift and empower,
    not compare and tear down   195

15. How we can be kinder online   211

16. Why we should be kinder to the planet   227

17. Why positive change happens
    in small moments   241

Acknowledgements   255

Glossary   257

References   263

INTRODUCTION

Hi, Benjy here! Welcome to my guide to kindness.

You're about to embark on a kindness learning journey with me, and before we begin, I want to remind you of one key thing: no one has all of the answers.

We are all human, and therefore imperfect – we often make mistakes, and that's OK. Because the world is a fast-moving, confusing place that can be tough to navigate at the best of times. It's impossible to know everything there is to know about anything, and there's always a new challenge around the corner.

This means that even the people who we all look up to, and trust to always do the right thing, are also figuring things out as they go along. They're maybe just a bit further along on their journey than we are.

So being the kindest person you can be takes a lot of courage. The courage to keep trying, keep making mistakes

1

and keep learning from those mistakes. The courage to keep showing up, with an open mind and heart, to try your best to do and be better.

Please see this book as a starter pack, providing helpful answers to some of the questions that are important to ask, when it comes to the topic of being kind. This will hopefully give you greater confidence and courage to ask more questions and continue to nurture your kindness skills on your own.

On our journey, we'll be learning why it's important to choose kindness and empathy, and the many ways in which we can be kinder to ourselves and those around us. This handy manual will equip and empower you with the tools required to start making a positive difference. To your life, the lives of those around you and the world.

If any terms seem tricky, there's a glossary at the back (see pages 257–262) that should come in useful.

Once you're finished, don't be afraid to return to a chapter if you need, and to share this book with someone else, to help them on their journey. Human beings are complex, but I believe that at our core, we all want to do right by ourselves, and others.

We just need some encouragement, guidance and kindness.

Ready? Let's begin!

I hope this helps.

1

Why should we be kind?

I magine if you were to witness an unfair exchange happen in a public place. You're shopping at a market, and while browsing a stall, you happen to see a woman be short-changed by the stall owner. The woman gives a £20 note for an item that costs £10 but only receives £5 back in change. The woman has a crying child with her and appears to be in a rush, so she doesn't notice what has happened and starts walking away. How likely do you think you would be to speak up and say something to the shop-keeper? Or further yet, run after the woman to encourage her to go back? Or maybe give her some of your money to make up for her loss?

The scenario described is based on a 2017 study that was conducted to research the extent to which the personality attributes of politeness and compassion influence the likelihood of people intervening as bystanders (Zhao et al, 2017). Participants were given a false scenario, in which they witness an unfair exchange between two people and have the option to use their resources to compensate the victim of the exchange. The study found that those who self-described themselves as being very strong in the personality attributes of politeness, honesty and active cooperation were no more likely than the average person to help the person who was short-changed. Not that they wouldn't react – but even though they possessed what most would consider to be strong moral attributes, they were still no more likely to act generously and compassionately than those who possess such attributes to a lesser extent. However, those who self-described as having more of a compassionate personality were significantly more likely than the average person to give more of themselves to compensate the victim.

Compassion means to 'suffer with', and is a kind, caring trait. I believe this difference in outcome highlights a powerful distinction, between what it means to be nice and what it means to be kind. Let me explain.

Kindness and niceness are often considered to be synonymous and are regularly used interchangeably in conversation. But while they are both positive attributes, they have different meanings. Being nice is akin to being polite and agreeable. When we think of nice people, they are usually people we like to be around because they are pleasing and aren't disruptive. Nice people are considerate of others and tend to go well with the flow, while being kind means that you show care and are a compassionate person. Kind people are people we can trust to do the right thing by us. These are very similar qualities, and you can be both kind and nice at the same time. They don't necessarily contradict each other. However, choosing to act in one way instead of the other does result in different outcomes.

The attribute of kindness is usually used to describe certain behaviours and actions, and when you think about it, kindness is very much rooted in action in a way that niceness isn't. For example, we have no qualms with describing inanimate objects as being nice. You could have a nice car for example, which is a car that looks appealing and is maybe of a reputable make. However, most would agree that it makes no sense to describe a car as being kind. To do so would be to anthropomorphise the car in some way.

What this highlights is that niceness, as a quality, is, to a certain degree, more static, shallow and less human than kindness. For example, many staples of common politeness are very much just niceties, and nothing more, because they lack a depth of authentic meaning. When someone sneezes, it is common in some places, including the UK, to say 'bless you'. This is a standard retort, regardless of whether you are familiar with the individual who has sneezed or have

7

a significant amount of genuine concern for their health and welfare. What might make such a response kind is if it were accompanied by a caring action. For example, if, in response to a sneeze, you replied, 'Bless you – would you like a tissue?'.

This difference also demonstrates that being nice is more passive than being kind. As you are essentially just going with the flow of what is expected and desired of you. Being nice doesn't require us to stretch ourselves or go above and beyond in any way. This means that niceness, though it has good intentions, can often fall short of being sufficient. Even if we are seen by others to have acted in a considerate way.

Let's say someone has invited you to their birthday party, and you can't attend for whatever reason – maybe you're busy, or you don't fancy their intended party plans. The nice thing to do might be to say yes and accept the invitation initially, while making plans to decline at the last minute, citing a family emergency. That way the person doesn't feel like they have been put out or rejected by you, and you can still maintain your relationship with them. However, this deceit is not the kindest or most considerate thing to do – which is to be upfront and honest. While this is more abrasive and potentially awkward, ultimately it means that the individual can plan accordingly and manage their expectations. In doing this, you are going beyond what your instincts may be telling you is the most expected thing to do and choosing to consider and protect the individual's welfare in the long run.

Niceness is motivated by perception and public opinion,

in a way that kindness is not. Because niceness requires us to follow certain social rules and customs, so we can be seen to fit in. For example, it can be both kind and nice to give up your seat for an elderly person on the train but only nice if the reason why you're doing so is that you're worried about what the other people in the carriage might think of you for letting an elderly person stand while you sit. I remember once having to get off a London Underground train because an older gentleman had declined my offer of a seat and decided to stand right next to me instead, as was his right to do. The glares that I received from other passengers who had not heard the gentleman decline my offer were too much to bear! Such social pressure is arguably intended to be caring but can be counterintuitive in practice. An authentically kind motivation would be to offer your seat because you can see the elderly person is uncomfortable standing and would like to offer them some respite – that's it.

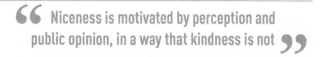

> 66 Niceness is motivated by perception and public opinion, in a way that kindness is not 99

To be kind is to be motivated to act in a caring way because you're driven by compassion, not social norms and selfish expectations. You want to do the right thing for the sake of doing so, not to improve how you're perceived or earn a certain reputation.

Niceness is also proper and well-mannered, in a way that kindness doesn't have to be. A desire to be nice could potentially stop you from telling a stranger coming out of the bathroom at a party that they have a sizeable train of dirty toilet paper stuck to their shoe. This is a pretty embarrassing thing to have to point out, for everyone involved, so you may simply choose not to bother in the hopes that they might eventually notice on their own or that someone else has the awkward conversation for you. The kind thing to do would be to go up to the stranger and just point it out. Arguably not the most refined interaction to have at a party, but the most compassionate thing to do for that person in the long run.

A desire to be nice can also stop us from being direct

when someone has done something to upset us or crossed an established boundary. In such situations, sometimes the kindest thing we can do for ourselves is be abrupt and sharp, so the message comes across and we can hopefully achieve a resolution.

That being said, being nice is not necessarily a bad thing. Sometimes it's caring to try to be nice, in the way that we are kind to others. It's caring to point out to the person with the toilet roll train that they have something stuck on their heel, in a nice way. Just to show consideration for their feelings, and not go excessively out of our way to make them feel self-conscious about their mistake. Niceness, in adherence to social norms, is also essential for social cohesion. We do need common standards and expectations, to a certain degree, so we can all have a meaningful understanding of what positive conduct is and how we can best coexist with each other. But it's important to understand the distinction between being kind and being nice, so we can ensure that we're being as kind as possible at all times. Because this is the best way to do the right thing for ourselves and for others.

Looking inwards, choosing to focus on being kind instead of being nice, allows us to become our most authentic selves, as niceness inspires inauthenticity. Because the behaviour and attitudes that are seen as nice are rooted in social norms and expectations, if we allow a desire to be nice to inform how we live our lives, we'll always be trying to be someone who others consider to be a well-fitting person. Rather than just being the most genuine person we can

11

be, for ourselves. We may even go so far as to suppress our authentic feelings and desires in the process of doing this, just to avoid disapproval. While being well-fitting is not inherently bad, we also need to prioritise our own interests to a certain degree. So we can do right by ourselves and not be a passive doormat at the mercy of people who may not have our best intentions at heart.

Niceness can result in people pleasing, which leads us to compromise our values, and ultimately who we are. It's also neither fun nor comfortable to feel like we have to pretend to be someone else and fit in a certain box all of the time. This can be hugely detrimental to our self-esteem and sense of self-worth.

Choosing to be kind means that we're pushing ourselves out of our comfort zone and into a place where we are open to trying new things and making mistakes. Because there isn't one set way to show care to others in every situation. Kindness requires an element of freestyling and, with this, also risk. However, such a risk can also result in a more compassionate outcome, so it is worth taking. Especially as making mistakes is the best way to grow, learn and become someone who is more equipped to take on the challenges of life. We simply gain more when we choose to be kind.

Being kind to ourselves also involves showing ourselves the utmost care by prioritising our wellbeing, regardless of how it may be perceived by others. This is therefore an essential act of self-preservation. Through the spirit of kindness, we can do things like setting healthy boundaries and non-negotiable self-care habits.

Looking outwards, prioritising kindness also enables us to be better to others in so many ways. For one, being overly nice can have a manipulative effect on others – one way this happens is through toxic positivity – the act of being optimistic and upbeat in every situation and circumstance and believing that others should do the same. People who are positive in such a toxic way are likely to provide empty reassurances to people's problems that are ultimately unhelpful, and discourage the discussion of difficult issues. We can fall into toxic positivity when we are too focused on being pleasing and artificially manufacturing nice environments instead of caring ones that are genuinely supportive. This has the effect of making others feel that they can't express themselves authentically and instead need to suppress their emotions or cope with their problems in silence.

Being overly nice is also a driver of the negative 'nice guy' trope that is often disparaged by women and those who have romantic interactions with men. The 'nice guy' is a man who feels that they are an incredibly decent person, especially compared to other men who are also dating, just because of how nice they are. They are usually not afraid to share this opinion of themselves openly and tend to list 'being nice' as one of their positive attributes to prospective suitors. This may seem like a strange thing to disparage, however, the implication of holding such an opinion of oneself and broadcasting it as a selling point is that you should therefore be rewarded. Or at least seen in a more favourable light when compared to others.

Being pleasant doesn't actually mean that you are going

above and beyond the call of duty or being a caring person in an especially admirable way. Rather it just shows you are adhering to certain social norms and not being actively harmful. Having such a focus on wanting to be seen as a nice person by others also indicates that you're not behaving in a genuine, authentic way, which is an obstacle to genuine connection. To truly connect with others, it's important to be yourself, so you can be appreciated for who you really are, as opposed to presenting a shallow version of yourself that you think people will like. This will, in time, ultimately be exposed for the deceit that it is by anyone who tries to peek behind the curtain and get to know you better.

Prioritising being nice can also stop us from doing the right thing and calling out harmful behaviour when we see it. It is often not pleasing or well-fitting to stand up for what is right – doing this sometimes means going against the grain or challenging the status quo. Being too concerned with how we're being perceived can cause us to stay silent when we see bad things occur. This can therefore limit our ability to help those who might benefit from our assistance and challenge the harmful norms that persist in our environments. Focusing on being kind liberates us, giving us the freedom and confidence to speak up.

When we focus on being nice, rather than kind, our actions have more potential to be transactional in nature. Because we're acting in a way that is intended to gain us social approval and acceptance from others, we are likely to be less motivated to help people who aren't able to give us that. For example, people who aren't as valued or approved of in our society, or who hold less power. Put it this way, we may be more likely to be nice to the CEO of a company we work at than the janitor, for example, if we are not concerned with being kind too. We also may be less likely to act in the nicest way possible if there is no one around to provide us with the social approval that we may be consciously or subconsciously expecting, or seeking, for our actions.

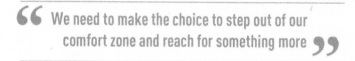

> ❝ We need to make the choice to step out of our comfort zone and reach for something more ❞

Niceness is not intrinsically a negative quality and it does have a valuable purpose. Nice actions are pleasant ones for a reason: they promote cohesion by improving social interactions and keep communities together. However, if we want to be active, positive forces for good, we need to make the choice to step out of our comfort zone and reach for something more. We need to be brave and speak up when no one else will, to go against the grain and do what is right for us and others.

To do that, put simply, we need to be kind.

2

Why it's not selfish to choose yourself

When thinking about what it means to choose yourself, my mind always goes back to a sign that I once saw above a community swap stand in Brighton. A swap stand is a designated area where members of the community can leave items that they no longer want or need for others to take. The sign above the stand had a list of rules for contributors to adhere to, including asking people to refrain from donating items in a bad condition, exploiting the system by taking too many items or leaving the stand in disarray. At the bottom was a call to action:

Please treat this place like it's somebody you love.

It warmed my heart, at the time, to see that the stand was indeed very well-stocked and impeccably kept.

The reason why that sign stuck with me is that it highlighted a principle that most of us hold to be true. Which is that the people we love deserve to have their wants and needs met and prioritised. Arguably our relationships with the people we love rely on this understanding. That, for example, if one is in a crisis, the other will help to the best of their ability. Or if we have something that the other needs, we will share it. We also understand that it's essential to uphold and support the dreams of our loved ones. We want them to be rested, fulfilled and happy, and we do what we can to help them achieve their goals.

That is ultimately what it means to choose and love yourself; to treat yourself like you're somebody you love. By trying your best to ensure that your wants and needs are met, and prioritising what makes you feel fulfilled and happy. Most would say that this is a simple, appealing principle. However, while it's something we may find easy to want for others, it can often be a struggle to want the same for ourselves. I believe there are a few key reasons for this.

The first is a desire to be perceived as being a nice person, as highlighted in the first chapter. To prioritise others is to please others. To give and share lots of yourself is often seen by others as being a positive quality because it's pleasing to them. We tend to like those who give things to us and so we are more likely to dislike those who choose not to – or at least we might appreciate them less. We may even label such individuals as being selfish because they are not freely giving of themselves, and we can sometimes perceive this as a disregard for others. It's therefore understandable why prioritising our needs can feel like a difficult task because doing so can put us at risk of being viewed unfavourably by those around us.

Related to this desire to want to be viewed as nice by

others is the pressure of cultural norms. My ethnicity is Ghanaian, and in many cultures, like my own, hard work and generosity are not just desirable qualities but expectations. They are requirements you need to adhere to in order to be accepted by the group. Some of my earliest memories are of our annual trips from London, where we lived, to our family in Ghana, with two suitcases each. One was filled with our belongings, the other packed to the brim with supplies for relatives. Shoes, food, clothes, you name it, we brought it. Not just that, but upon arrival, my parents would also be expected to give our relatives money. It was usually to help pay for school fees for my cousins (as most desirable schools in Ghana are not free) or for healthcare needs. These demands were based on an understanding that, as people who were living successfully in London, we had greater access and resources than our family back in Ghana. Therefore, the feeling was that this success should be shared – it was not just for the individual but for the group. The cultural desire for advancement and success also impacted me and my siblings as the careers that my parents desired for us were in the fields of medicine, law or engineering. We were steered towards industries with high-paying roles that would enable us to support our family in the future.

This cultural principle of giving selflessly and sharing to help the group can be a positive one. It instilled the importance of gratitude in me from a young age and the value of hard work. However, it can also lead a person who has been raised with these cultural values to have difficulty prioritising their needs and wants above others' because doing so may lead to ostracisation and disapproval. It's often a lot easier to go with our family's desires for us than it is to push against them and go our own way.

Societal norms can also present an obstacle to putting ourselves first. For example, in the case of gender expectations. Research indicates that women with children often lose job opportunities because of the common gender stereotype that says women should prioritise their children over their work once they become parents (Tabassum et al, 2021). Data also indicates that women in the US are the dominant primary caregivers and choose to leave their jobs after having children at higher rates than men do (Bhatia & Bhatia, 2020). You may have heard anecdotal evidence of this expectation placed on women when fathers describe caring for their children as 'babysitting' or people make light of men who choose to work in the home. Beyond being harmful to career progression, these gendered pressures can often lead women with children to consider themselves less worthy of prioritisation, and less able to choose themselves.

No matter the reason, and there are many more than I've detailed here, it's important to understand that putting ourselves first is not selfish – at least not inherently so. It is instead an act of kindness that furthers our ability to be kind to others. The example of oxygen masks on a plane is well-used to the point of cliché but it is undeniably true. In the case of a plane crash, we are of more use to those around us if we put our masks on first. Failure to do so means that we're likely to lose the ability to breathe before we're able to help anyone else – and that is the most important part of the analogy. Because choosing ourselves doesn't mean that we choose ourselves alone. It just means we choose ourselves first. The belief that prioritising one thing means we don't care about anything else is a harmful fallacy. We must choose ourselves first so that we can be of better service to others. It's impossible to pour from an empty cup.

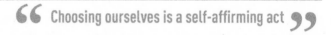

Choosing ourselves is a self-affirming act

In order to help a friend move house, we need to have had a sufficient amount of sleep the night before. In order to provide someone else with adequate emotional support, we need to be in a stable emotional state ourselves. In order to be patient with an angsty child, we need to be calm and centred ourselves. It's essentially a lot harder to be someone who others can lean on if we're unstable and at risk of toppling over at any moment. So choosing ourselves is, in many ways, the opposite of a selfish act – it's a necessary action to take, and one that can improve the lives of others around us.

Choosing ourselves is a self-affirming act. When we put ourselves first, we affirm our self-worth and send a message to those around us that we are worthy of prioritisation and care. This is part of having a radical approach to self-care. Radical self-care is a powerful practice to learn if we want to get better at putting ourselves first. Self-care is commonly understood to describe practices that enable us to improve our physical and mental wellbeing. Commonly proposed self-care practices often focus on us having a healthy diet, doing regular exercise and investing in stress management treatments like massages. You may think of people encouraging you to 'treat yourself' and 'be mindful' when you think of self-care. Those are all great, but radical self-care deliberately looks at self-care from a different angle.

The term 'radical' describes something completely new and different from the standard. When we talk about radical change, we're referring to change that comes from the root, and is transformative. Radical self-care, therefore, is an approach to self-care that seeks to be transformative and focuses on addressing the root causes of mental and physical wear, rather than fixing issues once they arise. This means considering how our health and wellbeing may be affected when making choices in our everyday life. Thinking critically about how we spend our time, our money, where we place our energy and what practices we implement at home and at work. It also involves having a revolutionary mindset and not being afraid to completely change how we do things if it means that we'll be valuing our humanity. The purpose of radical self-care is to encourage us to move from viewing self-care as a practice of indulgence to seeing it as an act of preservation.

Because arguably a typical approach to self-care is like only taking a car to the garage when it has issues that need fixing or when it's time for its yearly MOT. That may be a fine way to run a car, but the human body isn't a replaceable machine. If our car fails and is irreparable, we can buy a new one (if we have the resources to do so). But once our bodies break down, we can't just buy another body to live in. So, viewing self-care as an indulgent choice or a way to fix issues once they arise can therefore be detrimental to our wellbeing in the long-term, and is ultimately unsustainable. Instead, it makes more sense for us to think about what actions we can put in place to ensure we don't need an MOT in the first place. We need to place the prioritisation of our wellbeing at the heart of everything that we do and view it as an essential requirement, not a choice.

This approach to self-care comes from social justice movements. Between the 1960s and 1980s in the US, having a radical approach to self-care was a way for communities of colour and members of the gay liberation movement to affirm their value in a society that saw them as being lesser-than. For example, activists for racial equality such as Angela Davis and Ericka Huggins actively championed the use of yoga and meditation as a way for marginalised people to preserve their health. Famed poet and essayist Audre Lorde wrote extensively about how self-care was an act of political warfare. Their driving belief was that self-preservation was a necessary act for anyone living in a society that is hostile to their identity and community.

This is important as self-care holds a powerful group purpose. When we take the time to practice self-care and promote its importance, we uphold the value of our humanity and encourage others to uphold the value of theirs also. It's therefore important to do so in a way that is accessible and attainable by all, rather than commodified and exclusive. Everyone can try to make decisions that prioritise their wellbeing. Not everyone can afford to go on a luxury spa retreat when they are depleted.

There are some simple steps we can take in order to start applying radical self-care to our lives, and I'm going to share some with you here.

The first step is to say the word 'no' often. This is essential for putting yourself first, as in doing so, you affirm your boundaries and create space to be able to say yes to the things that will fulfil your needs and fill your metaphorical cup. I realise this is easier said than practiced. It's so much easier to say yes to others rather than saying no and facing the feeling that you're letting someone down. One effective tool that I have used to develop the skill of saying no is to create a 'no list'. This is a list of general rules and boundaries that I stick by. For example, to avoid burnout I have a certain number of work projects that I can take on in a month. I also have certain core values that I try to live by, such as being honest, not doing harm to others and seeking joy. Anything that doesn't fit with these, I say no to.

Having such a list to hand that you can refer to before making decisions helps identify what to say no to and also helps you to say no in a manner that is firm but kind, and also in a way that is understood clearly. For example, there is a difference between saying 'no – I don't want to take on this new project' and 'no – I can't take on this new project

as I am at the workload capacity that I have set for myself to avoid burnout'. Both should always be accepted but the latter clearly indicates that the decision has been made to honour your wellbeing, not to negatively impact others, and that the decision is not to be questioned. If you're just getting started with choosing yourself, I cannot recommend putting together such a list enough. It can help in so many situations, like when your manager keeps demanding too much from you, or you feel strained by the expectations of your family. Start by asking yourself questions such as: 'what are my key values and priorities?', 'what brings me joy?' and 'what are my non-negotiables at work?'

This brings me to the next step, which is to adopt non-negotiable habits that are specifically focused on fulfilling your needs. Think of activities you can do regularly to affirm your own value and ensure that you are happy and fulfilled. This could involve a morning fitness routine, having a long bath on Friday nights or a weekend every month that you exclusively spend by yourself. Doing so will make prioritising yourself part of your life and your routine and, as the saying goes, practice makes perfect.

I'd also recommend practising being grateful. To be grateful is to demonstrate appreciation. Practising gratitude regularly, therefore, means regularly showing appreciation for the good things in your life and acknowledging where they come from. Our brains can so easily dwell on the negative and the bad things, so it's about reframing and reconsidering what deserves our attention. Doing this often helps us to remember our intrinsic value, to find joy in our lives and therefore find purpose from within to practice self-care and prioritise ourselves. This is admittedly a tough one to do consistently. I've started many a gratitude journal with the best intentions, only to give up when life got busy, and I missed what I felt were too many days to make the task worthwhile. Or when I've had bad days when I couldn't think of a single positive thing to be grateful for.

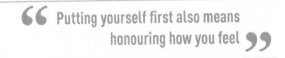

Putting yourself first also means honouring how you feel

So, I'd first say that *not* having a journal has helped me immensely. It doesn't work for me, and that's fine! I much prefer practising gratitude in my head while brushing my teeth before bed – so do what works for you. Having non-negotiable care habits also helps with this. For example, I have a non-negotiable commitment to myself, that I will never forget to eat lunch, no matter how hectic my schedule is. It's a tiny thing, but at least that's something I can note down and be grateful for.

I would also encourage you to look outside of yourself when seeking to be grateful, as you can often have a tunnel-vision approach to your day-to-day troubles and miss moments of joy and care. You can be grateful for the existence of the person who works at your local store, who asked if you wanted an additional bag to reinforce the one you've put your shopping in so it doesn't break on the way home, or you may even be grateful for the autosave function on that big work document that you've been immersed in. It really is the little things.

But putting yourself first also means honouring how you feel – and sometimes there are simply days when it's impossible to find the energy to be grateful, and that's also OK. We all deserve to give ourselves a break and accepting this is also affirming our value.

The final strategy I would recommend is utilising positive affirmations. These are short mantras that we can repeat to ourselves to remind ourselves of important principles. Doing this can change our perspective on life in an incredible way. One I use often is: 'I can, and I will.' Incredibly simple, but it has often given me the energy to pursue goals when I've lacked motivation.

Try this one. I use it to remind myself that it's not selfish to put myself first:

> *I choose me.*
> *I choose my happiness. I choose my peace.*
> *I choose me, so I can be the best me.*
> *For myself – and for the world.*

3

Why it's OK to change your opinion as you learn

'NORMALISE CHANGING YOUR OPINION WHEN PRESENTED WITH NEW INFORMATION.'

This is a slogan. I first remember seeing it written in bold on an Instagram post during summer 2020. It was a time of great uncertainty for most of the world. The COVID-19 pandemic caused every aspect of society to stand still, with millions forced to stay at home under strict lockdown measures to limit the spread of the deadly virus. At the same time, the news was filled with so-called 'COVID deniers'. People who either felt that the virus was an imaginary hoax, an intentionally engineered population control method or not worthy of concern. That summer also ignited a global conversation about racial injustice, following the filmed murder of African American George Floyd at the hands of police in Minneapolis, Minnesota, the latest in several such deaths involving law enforcement. Millions took to the streets in protest declaring that 'Black Lives

Matter'. Suddenly people were holding their friends, family members, employers and the institutions around them to account. Challenging them to confront racial inequality head-on, rather than choosing to turn a blind eye, and to do something to contribute towards racial parity and stop racism.

Both the pandemic and the focus on racism were catalysts for a forced reckoning. We all had to contend with the idea that the way we saw the world might not accurately reflect its reality. That maybe our right to roam freely, congregate in crowds, see our family and hang out with our friends could be taken away for valid reasons. That maybe not everyone had the same experience in society due to the colour of their skin. That racism was still very much alive and well.

Some took this information in their stride. Others chose to ignore it, or to push back in retaliation. We may say that those who fall into the latter group are being ignorant for reacting in this way. We may even deem their ignorance to be a valid reason for reproach and look down on them for not doing as the slogan on that Instagram post said. For refusing to change their opinion when presented with new information.

While I agree with the sentiment of this statement, I would also argue that ignorance is not a bad or shameful thing. It's a trait that unites us all and something we need to be more understanding of.

Let me explain.

To be ignorant is often seen as synonymous with being

a bad person, or someone who lacks intelligence. However, ignorance is not inherently negative, immoral or a reflection of how smart someone is. In literal terms, being ignorant simply means that we don't know something. We are therefore all ignorant, as no one knows everything there is to know about every topic, issue and subject in the world. Not only is the world vast, but it is constantly changing, along with the people that inhabit it. It's therefore impossible to be someone who doesn't lack knowledge. As the famous quote attributed to Socrates goes, 'I know that I know nothing'. Being uncertain is, arguably, one of the only certainties we have as human beings.

We are also all conditioned to be ignorant. Confirmation bias describes the human tendency to pay greater attention to information that aligns with the views we already believe to be true and seek this information out also. This is a phenomenon that is heavily researched and bears weight when applied to our everyday lives. Many of us have met the parent of a disruptive child who claims that they are just easily excited and well-meaning. Or have used the verified claims that red wine can be beneficial for the heart to justify ordering an additional bottle when out for dinner. It's an integral attribute of the human condition – to find safety in what we already know and want to believe.

There are even studies that indicate that our beliefs can hinder the speed at which we process information. For example, a 2018 study tasked participants to spot grammatical errors in sentences and found that people took longer to notice errors in the sentences that expressed opinions they disagreed with (Gilead et al, 2018). Our brains work better when dealing with information that resonates in an appealing way, irrespective of whether the information is flawed.

There are also many understandable reasons why someone may choose to remain ignorant.

For example, the aforementioned 'COVID deniers' could be experiencing a form of health anxiety. Those with health anxiety have extreme worries and fears about getting unwell, sometimes to a debilitating extent. While I would not diagnose myself with health anxiety, I do definitely feel uneasy when I enter a doctor's office, even if it's for a routine check-up. To me, hospitals are a place where people are highly likely to receive life-changing news, positive or negative. This, therefore, makes every doctor's appointment a potential threat to the stability of my world. Because I am afraid.

Fear is an emotion we all share, and one that can lead us to choose to be ignorant, even if we are aware that doing so will impact us negatively in the future. For example, choosing to deny the existence of the COVID-19 virus, because you're not ready for your world to change. Or turning a blind eye to a partner's infidelity because you're not prepared to deal with the pain of a breakup. Or refusing to check your bank account before payday, because you're scared of seeing how deep into your overdraft you are.

An interesting 2017 study demonstrated the extent to which we may be motivated to avoid information that we deem to be unpleasant, even if it goes against our best interest. The study gave participants the choice to read opinions, concerning marriage between couples of the same gender, with which they agreed or disagreed (Frimer, 2017). The incentive: if they chose the opinions they agreed with, they were entered into a draw to win $7, and if they chose the opposing opinion, they were entered into a draw to win $10. Incredibly, the majority of participants decided to read the opinion they agreed with, despite having a chance to earn more money if they didn't.

The amounts on offer arguably may have lacked appeal, however, the study still demonstrates the extent to which we can be driven to be willfully ignorant in order to avoid discomfort and distress. While I can appreciate the need to hear different perspectives before forming an opinion, as a Queer person, I'd be lying if I said that I actively seek out anti-Queer rhetoric in my every day.

It's also important to acknowledge that ignorance can be beneficial to us. For example, ignoring the information we don't know makes us confident in what we do know, and therefore more confident in our grasp on the world. As the saying goes, the emptiest barrels make the most noise. It's often less capable people that are the most self-assured, bolstered by a bravado that only ignorance can provide. This is actually a principle I used to get through my school and university exams, for which I was somehow always unprepared. Focusing on what we do know, and are good at, rather than wasting time and energy worrying about what we don't, can provide a self-assurance that is incredibly helpful. I have the grades to show for it.

Ignorance can also help us avoid what Barry Schwartz

calls 'The Paradox of Choice', which he unpacks in his book of the same name. The paradox describes how having increased numbers of options when making a decision is both desirable and detrimental. Desirable as most of us prefer to have options to choose from in life, so we may exercise our autonomy. However, an increased number of options can also be debilitating and stressful. If we have too many options to choose from, it's arguably difficult to be confident in our final choice, leaving us frozen with indecision or consumed by regret. Deliberately limiting our options can often be the kindest thing we can do for ourselves. For example, I personally find it a lot easier to shop when a brand runs a discount sale on certain items. Beyond the attractive discount, it takes considerably less effort to sort through a limited range than browsing through the store's entire catalogue.

Ignorance is therefore a justifiable and understandable universal trait. It's not something we should judge others or ourselves for, and it's not inherently negative either; it can actually be helpful. Acknowledging this is important, so we might engage with those who are ignorant about a certain topic or issue with kindness and compassion. We can also extend this same compassion and kindness to ourselves, if we are found to be ignorant, too.

However, we should still try our best to pursue awareness and encourage others to do the same. Because seeking out new information and ideas to inform our perspective and decisions is ultimately beneficial and important for ourselves and the world.

For example, consider the confidence afforded by ignorance that I touched on earlier. This may be helpful for getting through an exam after having done minimal revision or succeeding in a job interview with limited preparation. However, achieving an A in my English Literature exam doesn't mean that I have a full grasp of the syllabus. Or that I have benefitted from the entirety of the content that was taught. Similarly, succeeding in a job interview does not mean we have the capabilities to perform well in the actual role. A failure to acknowledge this could potentially result in a misplaced assurance that ends in disaster.

What I'm describing is also known as The Dunning-Kruger effect, which occurs when we are ignorant of our own ignorance, to the extent that we overestimate our abilities. This is the result of having a distinct lack of awareness, which lulls us into a false sense of security that can be swiftly pulled out from beneath us.

A personal example of this occurred in one of my first office-based jobs that I got while still studying for my undergraduate degree at university. When asked in the interview whether I was proficient in Excel, I enthusiastically agreed, waxing lyrical about my expertise in organising data and creating charts. In truth, I wasn't proficient, or even close to being so. But I did watch a ten-minute YouTube tutorial before my first day, which I assumed would be fine – how difficult could it be? You could imagine my horror when I was asked to organise data on my first day, using a function I'd never heard of before, with my new manager leaning over my shoulder. So embarrassing!

Beyond an awkward experience on the first day of a new job, ignorance can lead us to make wrong choices and hold harmful beliefs that have damaging consequences for ourselves and those around us. For example, a 2019 study from Yale University indicated that only 69% of people in the US believe that global warming is real (Yale University and George Mason University, 2019). This presents a harmful barrier to the issue of climate change being addressed in the US, as a significant portion of the population does not think it is a problem at all.

Ignorance can also be used by those in power with harmful intentions as a manipulation tactic. For example, the UK News International phone-hacking scandal of 2011. Journalists at the media company were found to have been engaging in nefarious tactics to get stories, to significant public outrage. Upon investigation, News International CEO Rupert Murdoch was able to successfully defer blame to his employees, claiming not to have been aware of the activities that were going on in his own company. Similarly, *The Ellen DeGeneres Show* came under fire, in 2021, due to allegations from the show's employees of harassment and bullying at the hands of senior staff. When questioned, Ellen, who fronts the programme, denied knowledge of these incidents, claiming to have learnt of them only from media reports.

The lack of awareness expressed by both Murdoch and DeGeneres is arguably a deliberate attempt to shirk account-ability by constructing a certain narrative. The denial of their awareness and therefore their involvement means that they are unconnected to the impact of their respec-tive scandals, therefore allowing them to retain power. In such situations, it is beneficial, if not imperative, that we, as critical outsiders, actively seek information. So that we can attain an accurate grasp of reality and hold the nec-essary people accountable for their actions. Being content to remain in the dark allows those with opportunity and intent, to leverage their power to serve their interests to the detriment of others. Achieving justice essentially requires awareness.

That is why, while being ignorant is not something to feel bad about, or judge others for, it's important that we all try our best to seek knowledge and aspire to be as informed as possible. This means being open to asking questions when unsure and challenging the beliefs that we hold, no matter how longstanding they are. It also involves being aware of the assumptions that we may hold about others and the world and trying not to act on them where possible. We can also enlist the help of others, by surrounding ourselves with people who have different experiences and perspectives than ours and asking them for feedback and insight on what we're unsure about. This is admittedly a lot easier said than done. Accepting information that conflicts with our existing worldviews can be uncomfortable, never mind actively seeking it out.

There are many truths that I wish I had been open-minded enough to accept at an earlier stage. From as serious and significant as my sexual orientation to as inconsequential as the fact that the afro I sported in my teenage years didn't suit me at all! I always knew both truths deep down, but it took me time to accept that they were my reality.

This difficulty is described by Jean Piaget as being due to the difference between the two ways we can process information. The first is *assimilation*, which is when the new information gained aligns well with what we already know to be true. So, for example, if I've gained a new friend who I am incredibly fond of, I'm likely to be able to easily accept it when they perform a nice gesture. I know them to be nice and genuine, so their action aligns with how I perceive them to be.

The second way Piaget argued that we can process information is through *accommodation*. This is necessary when we receive new information that contrasts with what we already know to be true. So, for example if my new friend does something that I take offence to or deem to be unkind. Processing this information will require me to adjust and change my original impression of my friend. As the information gained doesn't easily align with the information I already had. This is an uncomfortable feeling that requires more energy and effort. It can also be displeasing. This is why we may sometimes struggle to keep our minds open to learning new things about others, the world and even ourselves.

Accommodation is often required when we are accused of doing something wrong or holding a belief that is harmful, as most of us would like to believe that we are well-meaning people, with justified views. That we wouldn't intentionally act in a way that would harm someone else. So, when we do face such accusations, that contrast with the way that we view ourselves, this can push us to get defensive, to reject what is being suggested without considering it, in order that we don't risk changing how we perceive ourselves. While this is an understandable reaction, it is one that is detrimental in the long term. When we centre our own emotions and self-perceptions in such instances and focus on reacting, that leaves no room for *listening*. When we're not listening, it is impossible to learn and we open ourselves up to harmful ignorance.

When we find ourselves in such situations, it's important to try to fight against any defensive urges that may rise up, to choose to be open-minded and receptive to what is being said, instead. I often describe this as the choice we have to either take the loss or lose the lesson. The information that is being shared may not be justified or correct, but we need to be open to it – in order to judge whether this is the case or not. And this doesn't need to impact on our pride or how we view ourselves.

There is a way that we can help others process information better when the shoe is on the other foot and we are trying to inform someone who is ignorant on an issue. That is, to centre them, rather than us, in how we choose to educate. Often when we know more than someone about something, especially if we're confident about how right we are, we can unintentionally communicate it in a way that is patronising, therefore increasing the likelihood of getting a defensive response in return. I believe this occurs because our confidence causes us to make the conversation more about showcasing how much we know, rather than getting the other person to improve their understanding of our viewpoint.

An example of this is using overly complex language unnecessarily. When we're trying to explain something to someone with a more limited knowledge, it's not the best time to start sounding like we've swallowed a thesaurus. We should be trying to break things down into as simple terms as possible, without sounding condescending, to establish a foundation of understanding we can then build on. I'm also of the belief that if we're unable to break a complex topic down into simple terms, more often than not, this indicates a lack of understanding on our own part.

Another example is when we're sharing informative resources. Sending someone an extensive list of books that helped us understand a topic is only truly helpful if that person learns best by reading and has the time to read. Not everybody does. However, they may love watching TV or listening to podcasts, in which case it is probably possible to find an informative show or podcast that would be more helpful.

Remember that ignorance is not an inherently negative trait and that we all gain so much more by being open-minded, absorbing new information and allowing ourselves the freedom to change what we think and how we feel.

4

Why you shouldn't care what others think

Feeling we are disliked, or even hated by others, is rarely a pleasant experience. One of my earliest memories of feeling like someone had negative feelings towards me was at primary school, when I was eight years old. One of the most popular boys in my class had a birthday party and handed out birthday invitations on the playground to, what felt like, everyone in our class apart from me. We weren't exactly close, but I still remember my exclusion from his birthday event as being a huge shock to my system. Before that point, it was common for everyone to receive an invite to whoever's party it was, regardless of whether we were friends or not. But this boy's parents had decided that he was now old enough to have the autonomy to curate the invite list for his event – and I had been cut. It was the first time I had ever felt that the person I was might be displeasing to someone else, and it was hard to process. Little did I know that I was to have many similar experiences throughout my schooling, and beyond too – and while I would learn to process it better, it still wouldn't feel great.

This is why I have a difficult relationship with the 'haters are going to hate' rhetoric, that is the idea that we should all be able to cast the thoughts and feelings of those who dislike us to the side with ease because they don't matter. Being disliked sucks. And it's OK to admit that. For many serious reasons. For example, getting a feeling of dislike and hate from someone is often a precursor to a negative experience. Like the Saturday afternoon I had to spend at home all those years ago while my classmates enjoyed a party that I'd been excluded from. Or being shoved into the lockers at secondary school moments after an older boy insulted me about my weight. Or receiving racist abuse from a stranger on the bus home from a university night out after receiving an intense dirty look from them.

Being disliked or hated is often a sign that we're about to be put in an uncomfortable or dangerous situation, so it should naturally follow that this is an experience that holds significant weight and is therefore hard to shrug off with ease. Hate can also reinforce insecurities that we have about ourselves, causing us immense distress. Especially if it's coming from people we admire, or whom we perceive as holding authoritative power – like the popular boy in my primary school. This is a heavy burden that can be tough to shrug off.

However, it is also true that the kindest thing we can do for ourselves is to try our best to learn how to care less about the negative thoughts that others have about us. To care less about what people think about us. Unpacking the reasons why people hate is an important first step in understanding why this principle rings true, and how best to put it into practice.

As humans, arguably we have an innate capacity to dislike others that comes from our in-group/out-group instincts. What I mean by this is that we tend to prefer – and like to stick with – those we consider similar and identify with. This automatically makes those who don't fit into certain criteria, outsiders. People who we feel justified enough to like and trust less than those within our group. In prehistoric times, this was an essential survival tactic to facilitate the cooperation required to ward off any potential threats. But this innate instinct is still at play today. Children are a great example of this. Research indicates that two to four year olds, when pushed to do so, will favour those they perceive to be in their in-group, over behaving in a fair or more considered way (Lee et al, 2018).

Another example is football teams: think how passionately fans support their team when it comes to matches and tournaments, spending great effort on writing taunting chants about their opponents. The dislike and lack of trust generated by this instinct is just a side-effect of a positive desire for belonging and shared purpose. It feels great to be part of something bigger than ourselves – and have people around us we trust to have our best interests at heart. Having a shared dislike of another person or group – the 'other' – can often also strengthen the bonds we have with people in our group.

This in-group/out-group instinct can also make us vulnerable to developing prejudices against certain social groups, however. For example, arguably no one is born holding racist beliefs yet some are conditioned to hold certain opinions about others based on their race – either by what they hear from the people around them, their own culture and its alleged superiority or the media they consume. Some may also form their opinion on a whole social group, based on an experience they had with someone from that group. This may lead to prejudice, which is what fuels hate crimes – where someone seeks to target and hurt another person because of their identity.

Let's be honest. We're all human and hating others can also feel really good! Especially if you are in an unhappy place. If we are struggling with our own body image, for example, it can be really reassuring and satisfying to tear down how somebody else looks. In doing so, we can convince ourselves that maybe we shouldn't feel so bad about how we look, in comparison. Or we can at least make someone else feel bad about their body, so we're not alone in how we feel about our own. Misery loves company after all. Additionally, when things are going wrong in our lives, it can feel empowering to place the reason for this on someone else, so we can hate them for it. This takes us out of the hot seat, since we are no longer accountable. Sometimes this is unjustified – for example, hating people for not meeting our needs when we haven't taken the time to communicate what they are. But sometimes it is justified to a certain extent. For example, victims of hate crimes. Growing to hate those who have wronged them is arguably not a productive or healthy emotion, but perhaps one we can empathise with when people have had certain negative and debilitating experiences.

Hate can also be rooted in feelings of jealousy. Watching someone else live a life that we ourselves are struggling to achieve but desperately want can trigger strong feelings of resentment or bitterness. In the past, I've found myself subconsciously distancing myself from people in my life who have achieved great things when I've been in a bad place, even if I am genuinely proud of them. Jealousy is a natural emotion that we all feel at some point in our lives but it's key to let it pass over us and not dwell in it for too long. Or it can manifest into hatred.

Finally, we can also come to hate and dislike those who betray us. People often say that love is the sister of hate, this is why. When you invest significant time, energy and emotion in someone else, only for your contributions to be exploited or wasted, your positive feelings can quickly turn to negative ones. Arguably if you are completely ambivalent and unmoved after a loved one betrays you, this may indicate that your feelings may not have been as deep as you thought they were (or that you're still in love with them).

When we reflect on all of the reasons why we come to hate and dislike others, what quickly becomes clear is that they are all driven by personal motivations. This may sound obvious, but when we, for example, hate people who are part of a group that is dissimilar to ours, we do so because of how we personally feel about that group. Because of the experiences we've had and the beliefs that we may consciously or subconsciously hold. Our dislike is directed towards them, but the target is not involved, unless our hate spills over into action against them. Even if we hate those who have hurt and betrayed us, our hate is a reaction to their actions. Unless they have, for some reason, explicitly asked us to hate them, our dislike is very much an 'us problem'.

Therefore, when thinking about coping with receiving hate and being disliked, what is important is to understand that while we can try to influence the emotions others have towards us, we can never truly control them. We could try every day of our lives to try and convince someone who hates us to reconsider, but if they are committed to hate, they will continue to do so, regardless of any effort by us to stop it. Ultimately, we would be wasting our time and energy. And even if we were successful, that's just one individual out of potentially many.

I'm sorry to break the bad news, but it's true.

As someone who makes social media content for a living, I can tell you this from experience. I could say online that I love apples, and someone who is fervently anti-apple will immediately let me know that they disagree and that I have gone down in their estimation. I might then decide to go back on my previous statement, claim that I was being hyperbolic and that actually, I just mildly like apples and can empathise with those who dislike them, only then for someone who loves apples to let me know that they're disappointed in me. Never mind all of the people who are anti-fruit and completely turned off by this discourse entirely.

The point is that we can't please everyone: being disliked is an unfortunate reality for us all, one that we have no control over. Even the most beloved and influential historical figures, such as Mother Teresa and Dr Martin Luther King, Jr, are hated with a passion by some people, who have reasons that are very valid to them. And while it's understandable to feel weighed down and affected by hate and dislike when it's directed our way, dwelling on what we can't control won't change it.

It's also important for our wellbeing that we try our best not to give the negative thoughts of others any weight. Because when we give them weight, we give them power. This can quickly lead to self-hatred – internalised negative thoughts and beliefs about ourselves that are not true. This can have a disastrous destructive impact on our lives if we aren't able to shield ourselves. Confirmation bias means that we are more likely to readily focus on, and accept, whatever aligns with our beliefs. Meaning that if we start to internalise hate, we may start to then believe those negative thoughts, and therefore are more likely to internalise them even more. Ultimately making ourselves our own enemy whose harm it's impossible for us to evade.

So how do we put this into practice? How can we learn to care less about the negative thoughts of others, and let go of emotions we can't control?

Well, the first thing it is important to do is to critically self-question and consider whether we are receiving hate in the first place. We are all the centre of our own universes, and rightly so. I am the Beyoncé of every room that I walk into, and I dare anyone to tell me otherwise. However, because we're all so focused on ourselves and our own experiences, it can sometimes be easy to frame every situation in a way that makes us the focal point. For example, if you have plans to meet your friend for a coffee and they cancel at the last minute it would be easy to take it personally and assume that their actions reflect how they feel about you. This could be true, of course, but there may also be many other possible reasons for why they have cancelled at the last minute, such as a family emergency or a personal health scare. There could also be reasons that they're not comfortable disclosing yet. It's important to have boundaries and expectations in relationships but it can be unhelpful to jump to our first conclusion. It's better to try and rationalise such situations in an objective way and consider other possibilities. Yes, someone could have made a hurtful remark about a new hairstyle you're trying out because they dislike who you are as a person. Or they could have misused their words or been having an off day. That doesn't change how that remark made you feel, the impact is still the most important thing. Yet considering that there may be other reasons for someone's negative actions that aren't rooted in hate can empower you to handle the situation without incurring as intense a knock to your self-esteem.

Conversely, what we consider to be hate could actually be criticism that we should consider taking on board. It's important to learn how to recognise the difference. Criticism isn't always nice or pleasant. Often someone who is being critical of us, our lifestyle or work may choose to be explicit and direct to get their point across. So, it's understandable that this could rile us, triggering defensiveness. Yet criticism can be *constructive* rather than *destructive*, hard to hear but intended to help us grow or change for the better. For example, I am not exactly the greatest chef in the world. While I do enjoy cooking on occasion, it's not one of my greater strengths. There have therefore been a few times when I've made meals for friends who are significantly more skilled in this area, and received kind, but direct feedback from them on what could be improved. This understandably doesn't feel great, but their comments are intended to help me improve a skill that they know I lack competency in. It's therefore in my best interest to try and take their points on board.

> 66 I am the Beyoncé of every room that I walk into, and I dare anyone to tell me otherwise 99

Hateful comments are the ones that have no genuine care for our development and wellbeing. Instead, they focus on being unkind and tearing us down. Hate holds no beneficial value for us, yet criticism, when intended with good heart, may be an attempt to convey something of value that could be helpful in certain circumstances. Criticism should also ideally come from someone who has the necessary authority and perspective to truly understand what they are commenting on. So, when we receive what we perceive as unfavourable feedback from others, it's always important to take a moment to consider who it has come from and whether what they've said could be helpful or have good intentions behind it.

If you have done your due diligence and are genuinely experiencing true dislike and hatred, I suggest following my six essential guidelines on how to cope with receiving hate:

1. *Allow yourself to feel upset.* We are human beings, not robots – and to be human is to have emotions. Receiving hate can have a serious impact on our mental and sometimes physical wellbeing, so it is unrealistic to expect to be able to shake it off without any detrimental impact to ourselves. So, feel sad and hurt if you need to, hold space for your authentic emotions. Cut yourself some slack.

2. *Create distance if needed.* Often the most helpful and effective thing we can do to deal with hate is to remove ourselves from the situation. Remember that

hate and dislike are personal emotions that may be directed towards us yet are ultimately out of our control. So, choosing to engage with someone who is expressing hate towards you is often a futile, fruitless task. Choose yourself in such situations. Remove that person from your life, temporarily or permanently, if need be. Protect your peace at all times.

3. *You don't have to be gracious.* Do not be the 'bigger person' at the expense of your emotional energy and wellbeing. If someone is choosing to direct hate towards you, try your best to be kind, but you don't *owe* them niceness. So don't be afraid to be direct and firm if need be. When they go low, put yourself first and get the keys to the basement.

4. *Take accountability, if needed.* While we shouldn't waste our energy by trying to change the opinions of those who hate us, it can be productive to consider how we have contributed to them feeling that way. Is there an aspect of our behaviour that we could change in the future? Have we genuinely caused someone else harm? These are important questions, so ask yourself what you would think about the situation if someone else was in your shoes and you were making an outsider assessment. We can sometimes pull positive learnings from negative experiences to fuel our personal growth and development.

5. *Stay in your lane.* No one knows who you are or your purpose in life better than yourself. Therefore, the opinion on your life that you should value first and foremost is your own. Hate is inherently destructive and it will always be to your detriment to let negativity dictate how you live your life. So be self-aware and self-critical – both are necessary for growth – while remaining firmly on your chosen path and focusing on your larger mission and purpose.

6. *Accept that you are not for everyone.* Remember that if you say you like oranges, someone will hate you for not showing enough affection towards pears. You are a unique individual who will never be to everyone's tastes, and rightly so. Because it's impossible to appease everyone without distancing yourself from who you truly are. So, the kindest thing that you can do for yourself is to become comfortable with the possibility of being hated by some, while remembering that this also means that you are loved by others. Seek those people out. Surround yourself with kind people who love you, have your best interests at heart and don't need to be convinced to show love towards you. Keep your face turned to the sun always. Because nothing grows in the dark.

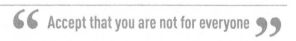
" Accept that you are not for everyone "

5

Why impact means more than intent

I magine this.

You're sitting on a park bench, reading a book, when someone walks past you, drinking a coffee. They trip on a crack in the pavement and stumble, spilling coffee all over your book in the process. The person then continues walking. You exclaim: 'You've ruined my book!' To which they reply, 'But I didn't mean to!' And keep going. This may make you feel upset, or at least annoyed. But why? The person is right: they didn't mean to trip; it wasn't their fault.

Yet, the person just focused on why they tripped and not what happened to your book. That's why you're upset. To be kind to others, we need to consider the impact of our actions, not the intent behind them.

Our intentions are the effect we want our actions to have. They are usually a reflection of our personal motivations, the beliefs we hold and our personalities. Our intentions are inherently tied to the people we are, and we have control over them. To act with intention is to be purposeful and focused about how you move through the world.

Our impact, however, is the actual outcome of our actions, which is influenced by but unfortunately separate from our intentions. We can try our best to predict what will happen, but this is never completely within our control. Even in the case of dealing with seemingly inanimate objects, anything could happen. You could try to dig a small hole in the ground and end up somehow bursting a pipe by accident. Human beings are even more unpredictable: when interacting with other people we have almost no autonomy over how they will react. In most cases, our impact on others is influenced by their beliefs, personalities and own motivations. The only way we can gain further influence on our impact on other people is through further action.

When there is a disconnect between our intent and impact, this can lead to a positive intention of ours creating a negative result. If so, we are likely to be faced with disruption and conflict and results we didn't originally anticipate Sometimes such a harmful disconnect comes from simple human error. Like the person with the coffee, in the aforementioned scenario, whose intention was simply to walk by while continuing to enjoy their beverage. In other situations, such a disconnect can occur because the things we say or do just aren't received in the way we intended them to be. Perhaps because of an interpersonal difference in background and opinions. Perhaps because we've misspoken and said something offensive unintentionally.

Perhaps because we've failed to communicate or act with adequate clarity.

No matter the reason, it's important to recognise and acknowledge that our impact means more than our intent, so we should act accordingly. If someone has, for example, expressed offence at a comment we've made, jumping to share our positive intentions behind the comment doesn't erase the harmful impact we've caused. It may help them understand us better, but it doesn't change the outcome: we have still offended them. Saying that we didn't mean our comment to be offensive doesn't cancel out the hurt and is also dismissive of the person's feelings.

This is sometimes hard to accept if we genuinely have had the best of intentions – especially if, for example, the comment was meant to be taken as a sincere compliment. Regardless, when someone brings to our attention that we have had a harmful impact on them in some way, we need to accept this and not be defensive. They are asking us to take accountability for the outcome of our actions, that's all, and this is something we are responsible for.

However, this also doesn't mean that we should take such allegations as an attack on the quality of our character or assume that they are calling us a bad person. Not everyone has the same perspective and opinion as us, so we are likely to encounter people who disagree with or don't understand us. We are also just human, so are bound to make mistakes.

Misunderstandings and conflicts are a part of everyday life that we just have to contend with and just because we have caused someone harm or offence, it doesn't mean we are bad people. Jumping to such a conclusion can cause us to get defensive, which is, in itself, harmful. Reacting this way when someone points out how we've harmed them implies that we are more concerned about being perceived as a bad person, than considering how we treat others. We are centring ourselves and prioritising our feelings over that of the affected person when we do this. Thinking about our character in such a binary way can also stop us from growing as people, as not everything is simply bad or good. Having healthy interactions with others involves navigating the subjective *greys* of human emotion. Sometimes we get it right and sometimes we don't. And that's OK.

When we do get it wrong and we're called out, the best course of action is simply to listen. To try to take in and understand how the other person is feeling and how we have hurt them. To take a look at what has occurred through their eyes and take accountability for our actions. To apologise and make amends.

There are also ways that we can work on being more aware of and responsible for the impact of our actions on others. The first is to try to always act in a way that considers the impact of the things we want to do. To get into a regular habit of doing this, before we say or do something. To take a moment and slow down. Make space to critically consider how our actions will be received. The more we do this, the more natural it will become.

For example, in our day-to-day life, we may experience a desire to comment on someone else's body that comes from a sincerely well-meaning place. Maybe because we're concerned about their recent weight gain or weight loss, want to know if they're pregnant or just want to say that we think their body is looking great. Without taking a moment to think, we could make the comment, only to receive a negative reaction.

Because while our intentions may be positive, unless the individual has asked, or we're in an environment where everyone has accepted that talking about bodies is OK, it's always kinder to keep such comments to ourselves. We never truly know the relationship people have with their bodies, or the physical or mental struggles that they may be going through. For many, bodies are a sensitive subject and comments can come across as overly intrusive and be harmful to their wellbeing, even if they are meant positively.

With this in mind, in such a situation, it may be kinder to say something positive about that person's general spirit, or the energy that they bring to the room. Then let them comment on their body if they would like to. As an example, you might say: 'You are glowing today'; or, 'You seem happy/ confident.' This is a kinder choice that you will be more likely to make if you stop to consider what the potential outcome of your comment might be. This is a habit that is worth cultivating.

Another way that we can improve our awareness of our impact is to try our best to have open and honest dialogues with the people in our lives. Misunderstandings are often a result of miscommunication, which results in our actions being interpreted in a different manner than how we originally intended. When we have more optimum channels of communication with those around us, confusion is less likely to occur.

This also helps create space for people to safely challenge us and hold us to account, if needed. We can then take on board learnings from those experiences and use them to inform our future behaviours. In a similar vein, it can also be helpful to try and surround ourselves with different types of people who have varying perspectives from our own. This is a way of getting used to being received in different ways and breaking down any assumptions we may have about what is and isn't harmful to say and do.

It's also helpful to try and be more sensitive to the feelings and emotions of others, if you can. Not everyone is able to pick up on social cues and mood shifts, but if this is something you're able to become more attuned to, it will definitely help.

Consideration of context is also useful to keep at the back of our minds at all times. We are more likely to be understood by those we are closest to, as we are more likely to share the same values. That is why friendship groups will have certain in-jokes that are understood, within the group, as being humorous in intention and therefore also in impact. However, such jokes may be deemed offensive by those outside the group, who are not aligned with the same values and understanding the members have. We, therefore, can't use the fact that the joke is acceptable in the in-group as a defence for using it outside of the group. Context matters.

Consider where you are, who you are around and how

that may influence how your actions are received. This doesn't mean that you shouldn't be your most authentic self, but rather that you should try to do so in a sensitive way, if possible.

Understanding the difference between intentions and impact, and why impact means more, helps us to understand each other better and be kinder to one another. When we take responsibility for our impact, regardless of our intent, we can also learn, grow and work towards having our intent and impact more often authentically align in positive ways.

6

Why it's important to understand our privilege

Our identities are central to who we are as people and how we experience the world. As a child of Ghanaian immigrants to the UK, I've always been acutely aware that while my nationality may be British, my ethnicity is very much Ghanaian. My ethnicity influenced how I saw myself growing up, and how I still view myself today. I share two distinct cultural lenses equally, British and Ghanaian. I'm just as likely to be a stickler for queuing, like a proper Brit, as I am to do anything I can to avoid handing someone an object with my left hand, like a Ghanaian (this is seen as a sign of disrespect in our culture). Beyond this, my experiences growing up were always undeniably Black. For example, most Black people reading this will know about 'the look'. For those who don't, Black or otherwise, I'll explain.

As a Black person, at least from my experience in London, when you pass another Black person in the street, it's customary to shoot them a knowing glance, or nod. Not so eager to the extent that it comes across as overfamiliar, and not so long that it's invasive, but just friendly enough to convey a certain reassurance.

It's a singular glance, which with no words says something along the lines of: 'I hope you're all right'. It's not something anyone teaches you, it's just something you wake up one day and start doing, maybe from seeing others do the same. Thinking about where this comes from, I'd hazard a guess that it's an acknowledgement that while we are all individuals, we share a common experience that comes with its unique challenges.

This, of course, isn't a uniquely Ghanaian or Black thing. There are many visible and invisible aspects of all of our identities that can influence our experiences. For example, being disabled, being shorter than average, being raised in a single-parent household or growing up in an area that has good schools. All of these things, and more, influence how we engage with the world and how the world receives us; they are a part of what makes us unique as people.

There are certain identities that, historically, have held dominance over others that still exist today. In Western society, this would include social groups such as White people, cisgender men (cisgender, or cis, means that you identify with the gender you were assigned at birth) and those with significant wealth, among other identity groups. What is meant by dominance is that such groups have held substantial power and this has enabled them to make decisions that impact on others, influence social norms (i.e. what is considered acceptable and unacceptable), and also create systems that benefit them and affirm their power. We can see evidence of this in Western society today within the policies, systems and structures that govern our society and prioritise the needs of people who hold certain identities. In doing so, they disadvantage, disenfranchise and oppress other social groups that are less dominant, for whatever reason. Because it's impossible to hold power without someone else lacking power. Those lacking power, or those who are powerless, are the groups that are on the other side of the metaphorical coin – including People of Colour (POC), women, members of the LGBTQIA+ community and those of low-income status.

Holding a dominant identity – like being a White, cis man – is what is meant by having social privilege. It's specifically a privilege because the identity you hold allows you to benefit from imbalances of power in society. This means that your experiences are informed not just by your identity but also by the unearned advantages that you have because of the identity you hold, which aren't afforded to others.

This can be a tough principle to get your head around when you are just thinking about your own experiences. As a cis man myself, it's difficult to consider the idea that my existence as a man may somehow be supercharged by these invisible benefits. Yet while it's impossible to ignore that being a woman or trans individual in society comes with its challenges, being a cis man isn't always a walk in the park either, trust me.

But this is arguably because the advantages that are

afforded to me as a cis man are essentially 'baked in'. As a cis man, most of society has been built with my gender in mind. From a gender perspective, I'm playing the game of life on the default setting – no adjustments or updates are required. When you live this way, it can be hard to comprehend that others have to make certain adjustments. Even when you do, you're more likely to see certain obstacles others face as being personal problems that may even be their fault – as that is the experience of privilege. As the default, you are afforded the benefit of being treated as an individual, because your identity isn't necessarily special, so it's likely that you may think that others have the same experience too.

Having privilege can also be difficult to accept because it goes against the general principle of meritocracy that we're fed from childhood. That we all have the same twenty-four hours as Beyoncé, and if you try hard and put in the work, you can achieve anything that you want to in life. The notion that everything we achieve is down to our own merit is satisfying and makes the everyday struggles of life that we go through seem worthwhile. However, it's an illusion – it's simply not true.

For example, let's unpack the most infamous of privileges to have – White privilege, which describes the unearned advantages that you get as a White person. These privileges are afforded to White people because Western society is informed in all areas by White supremacy, which is the belief that the thoughts, actions and needs of White people are superior. For generations, people with power have made choices based on this belief, therefore creating a societal structure that is designed to disadvantage People of Colour. As a White person, this privilege is afforded in lots of little everyday ways that you may not consciously consider. For example, being able to turn on the TV, open a magazine or vote in an election and not have to be concerned with the fact that you won't see yourself represented. Or going to a make-up counter and being confident that you will find your shade of foundation in stock. Or missing out on a work opportunity and not having to worry that you may have lost it because your race was judged to supersede your capabilites. The reverse of all of the aforementioned examples are common, everyday experiences for People of Colour.

Beyond the everyday, a lack of privilege significantly impacts the life chances of People of Colour. For example, in the UK, data indicates that Black women are five times more likely to die from childbirth than White women; women from Asian ethnic groups are twice as likely (British Medical Association, 2020). While there may be many contributing factors to this statistic, this still highlights a significant dis-parity when it comes to the experiences that People of Colour have within our health system. There is no biological reason why they should be dying at such a greater rate. The COVID-19 pandemic also had a disproportionate impact on People of Colour, with all minority ethnic groups facing a higher risk of death than White people (British Medical Association, 2020). This is a statistic that's again, informed by many factors, one of which is the way in which British society is structured. People of Colour, in the UK, are (and were) more likely to work in jobs that expose them to the virus, due to a persistent lack of opportunity when it comes to office work. For example, a third of taxi drivers and chauffeurs in the UK are Bangladeshi or Pakistani (British Medical Association, 2020). A similar situation is found across the Atlantic, where African Americans were being hospitalised and dying at a disproportionately higher rate than White Americans, in 2020, at the height of the pandemic (Vox, 2020). White privilege is not just about being able to easily purchase a skin-tone plaster at your local pharmacy. In many situations, it's the difference between life and death.

We can also talk about the gender privileges given to cis men, as mentioned earlier. This is afforded by the patriarchy, which describes a system that has been designed to provide men with power, while excluding women and trans individuals from it. This creates a hierarchy that places men at the top, in all areas of life. As recently as the twentieth century, this privilege marked the difference between being able to own a bank account, buy property, pursue higher education and vote in elections. While this may seem like a thing of the past, women and trans individuals are still, in many ways, tussling for their autonomy today. As a cis man, you are less likely to face societal pressures to have children at a certain age and if you do have children, it's less likely to affect your career. Societal standards of beauty affect you less as you get older, and, as a cis man, you face significantly less judgement and disapproval for showing your nipples in public (context depending of course!).

Meanwhile, the right for women to terminate unwanted pregnancies is one that is constantly up for debate, the recent overturning of *Roe vs Wade* in the United States, and its impact on reproductive rights for US women, highlighting this. Women all over the world are unable to exist without fear of harassment and abuse from men who feel that they have the right to do so, who feel they have ownership over women's bodies simply because of their gender. This continued attack on the bodies of women, and trans individuals, means that it is impossible for them to live lives completely devoid of fear. This is a power dynamic and just one of many ways that a lack of gender privilege can be detrimental in the society we live in.

Another form of privilege that holds significant weight in Western society is being cisgender and heterosexual. This is due to *heteronormativity* – the belief that heterosexual attraction and relationships are the norm – and *cisnormativity* – the belief that being cisgender is the normative gender identity to hold. Western society is informed by these beliefs, therefore disadvantaging anyone who isn't heterosexual or cis. Holding such a privilege means that you never have to justify your gender expression or who you choose to love because both are seen as being the expected standard.

It is so intriguingly strange to me when I see parents dress a boy in shirts and call him a 'ladies man', or encourage their girl child to have a play 'boyfriend'. Beyond the questionable sexualisation of children, it's a huge signifier of the extent to which many see being heterosexual and cis as the default. So much so, that they would place these identities on their progeny before they are old enough to affirm their sexual orientation and gender identity for themselves. This is not to say that the intent behind such actions is always harmful – in fact, I'd guess that in most cases it's not. However, for people like me, who do have gender identities and sexual orientations that are different from what is seen as the norm by so many, this places a heavy burden on us to have to come out and declare who we are in the hope of acceptance. The coming out experience is different for everybody, but it's a myth that it only happens once. As someone who isn't cis or heterosexual, you face having to come out many times in your life, often to complete strangers.

This is not only a vulnerable, emotionally intensive experience but can also lead to detrimental life outcomes. A 2021 US study found that over one in four LGBT (lesbian, gay, bisexual, transgender) people reported experiencing at least one form of employment discrimination in their career (being fired or not hired) due to their sexual orientation/gender identity (School of Law Williams Institute, 2021). Similarly, a 2021 UK study found that 40% of LGBT people had experienced a conflict at work relating to their identity in the past year, such as being verbally abused, feeling undermined and humiliated or being directly discriminated against (CIPD, 2021).

Another privilege that significantly influences your experience is that of not being disabled. This is due to *ableism*, which describes the assumption that disabled people are not the standard and are less valuable than those who aren't disabled. Our society is informed by this belief, meaning that the needs of the latter are catered to first and foremost, excluding disabled people in the process. This results in a significant lack of accessibility for disabled people, to an extent that you may not consider until you take a moment to think about everything you take for granted as a non-disabled person.

Think about public transport. I have managed to live through the majority of my twenties in London without a driving licence or car due to the incredible transport system that I benefit from. However, only around half of the tube and train stations in the city offer step-free access, making many parts of the city inaccessible for those with mobility aids that don't allow them to use steps (Transport for London, 2021). Inaccessible design, in general, is a huge disadvantage for disabled people. Next time you are at work, or in a restaurant, think about how the environment caters to you but may disadvantage others. From counter heights to the availability of ramps, lack of text-to-audio features or Braille on menus. These are all things that can and should be requested if they aren't available, and yet viewing the needs of disabled people as 'extras' is, in itself, ableist. Not having to think about these things is a huge privilege that cannot be denied.

I would encourage you to think about other parts of our identities that may afford us privilege. For example, wealth. One in five households in the UK are living in relative poverty (Social Metrics Commission, 2019).

Being low-income doesn't just impact your ability to feed and dress yourself or pay for your housing though, it also means that a significant portion of the population is unable to access or make adequate use of opportunities that can help us get ahead in life. From school trips to studying abroad at university, and even moving to a new city to tap into more lucrative job markets. The chart below is taken from a study conducted across 5,000 of Britain's elite (as defined by those in jobs that provide significant power, influence, prestige and

82

wealth). Professions include judges, business leaders, pop stars and sportspeople. It is clear to see that such elite fields are disproportionately dominated by those who attended fee-paying, independent schools. So, no matter who you want to be in life, the income level of the household you grew up in has a huge influence on your chances of getting there.

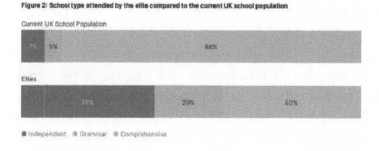

Figure 2: School type attended by the elite compared to the current UK school population

Source: 'Elitist Britain 2019' – Sutton Trust & Social Mobility Commission, 2019.

There are also many other privileges that we can often take for granted – like having an accent that is local to where you live or having English as your first language if you're in an English-speaking country.

So all things considered, it's clear that we don't all achieve everything that we have in life purely on our own merit. There are so many things that may mean that we have had a head start or an extra hurdle in our way compared to others. However, this doesn't mean that privilege is a neutraliser of hard work or dedication. No matter what privileges you hold, we can all still work hard in our own way to achieve the things that we want in life.

Acknowledging that you have certain privileges doesn't mean that you can't be proud of your accomplishments, or that the good things in your life are somehow underserved. In fact, acknowledging privilege is about affirming the exact opposite – that everyone deserves to have equal access and opportunity to achieve what they want to in life if they work hard for it. But unfortunately, this just isn't the case for everyone. That doesn't make those with privilege somehow bad people or villains – most of us are privileged in some way and that doesn't reflect the quality of our character. It just reflects how our identity is perceived, and how members of certain groups are treated in society.

Privilege also isn't a superpower. Being White doesn't automatically mean that you have a better quality of life than every Person of Colour, or that you are immune from struggle. The majority of people living in relative poverty in the UK are White and am sure wouldn't appreciate the assertion that White people do not struggle due to privilege (Social Metrics Commission, 2019). But that is not what privilege is about. Holding privilege just means that there are certain obstacles others face that you don't. But just because your path is free of certain obstacles, it doesn't mean that others won't fall in your way – sadly, life is often unpredictable and unkind.

In addition, holding privilege doesn't mean that you can't experience prejudice. Members of dominant social groups can still be put down and mistreated by others because of their identity, and this is something that we should all have empathy towards. Holding privilege doesn't justify mistreatment. The discussion of privilege is not about actively trying to disadvantage those with power and make them feel bad. It's about acknowledging the state of the world as it is, so we can work towards creating a society where everyone can get and make the most of the opportunities they want, and receive the support they need.

That's where you come in! Me, too – and anyone who holds privilege in some regard. Holding privilege is a beneficial thing for the world, as it gives us the ability to open doors for others and work towards making things fairer for all. We can use our excess power for good. But this can only happen when we face up to our privilege. This can be tough, as it takes some brutally honest self-reflection. But it's worth the work, as we also benefit ourselves when we do so.

You see, tapping into the privileges that society affords members of certain social groups also often means that you have to fit into limiting ideas about who members of that social group are. You have to fit the mould, so to speak, in order to have value and worth, even as someone who may have been born with privilege.

For example, being a cis man. The system of patriarchy also pressures men to conform, as only certain types of men are valued to the extent that they are afforded power. This is what is often coined as 'toxic masculinity' and includes attributes such as being strong, tall, tough and having financial power. These are essentially superfluous standards that people with power have deemed as indicating who is a 'real man' and who isn't. Fitting into such a limiting box is unrealistic for most and impossible for some, and with this comes stress and anxiety. These pressures can stop cis men from being their authentic selves, and I can attest to this, speaking from experience.

Being aware of the privilege we have, how it works to uphold some while oppressing others and, most importantly, how it is entirely constructed, provides us all with freedom. The freedom to be our authentic selves and to work on enabling everyone around us to do the same.

7

How we can be better
to each other

One of my favourite karaoke songs is 'Absolutely Everybody', which is an absolute (pun intended) anthem by Australian singer Vanessa Amorosi. If you're not familiar with the unofficial song of the 2000 Sydney Olympic Games, this flawless piece of nineties/noughties dance-pop magic is all about the value of togetherness. Over an up-tempo party beat that soundtracked many of my school discos, Vanessa sings about how there is no one in the world who doesn't need another person, so we should try our best to show love to all. This is a sentiment that's not too dissimilar to the Christian golden rule that I also had drummed into me growing up, to treat others how you would like to be treated. No matter your religion (or taste in nineties/noughties pop music) this is a simple yet potent idea. As members of our respective communities on this planet, the choices we make and the lives we lead will have an impact on others, whether it's directly or indirectly. It's therefore in our best interest to try to ensure that the impact we have on those around us is positive, in the hope that they'll return the favour.

I believe that an important way we can all try our best to be better to 'Absolutely Everybody' is by taking the time to unpack our respective privileges. This is so we can then use them in service to those who may be disadvantaged in ways that we're not. Because if you hold privilege in some respect, whether it be race, gender, sexual orientation or otherwise, you are benefitting from an imbalance in power. Being a beneficiary of such an imbalance means that you have the ability to play the role of an enabler. The decisions you make and the things you say hold influence, can drive positive or negative outcomes for others and make things possible that weren't possible before.

The act of harnessing power from privilege to support others is what is commonly described as allyship. That's essentially when we each take the time to be aware of, and responsible for, our personal influence, power and impact. Before strategically considering how we can contribute towards the betterment of those who face certain obstacles and the correction of power imbalances. So, for example, if you are a White person, benefitting from White privilege due to the pervasiveness of White supremacy and racism, you may use this privilege in support of those who don't have this privilege, i.e. People of Colour.

The discussion of White privilege and allyship is arguably the most common regarding using privilege in a positive way. But privilege can come in many forms, so there are therefore many ways that we can all be allies. For example, if you benefit from a higher-than-average income, this is a privilege that may be used in support of those who are of low-income status. Or if you aren't disabled, this is a privilege that can be used to help challenge ableism and support disabled people.

However, it must also be remembered that the extent to which privilege affords power is contextual. So having a privileged identity doesn't always mean that you have the ability to correct disparities. For example, if you are a White person working at a junior level in a racially homogeneous company, White privilege will only get you so far in trying to address the lack of racial diversity. You are still constrained to a certain extent by the power structures of your company. However, there are things you may be able to do. This might look like helping to advocate for your teammate who is the only POC in your department or reaching out to POC who want to get into your industry and helping them with their CVs or cover letters. That's why it's important to self-reflect before we think about how we can support others and consider the tools we have in our respective arsenals. What is our current social positioning, and how can we best leverage this in the service of those who need it most?

This is work that is impactful. A 2021 report found that when women feel that they have strong allies at work, they are 65% more likely to be happy with their job (McKinsey & Company and LeanIn.Org, 2021). They are also 40% less likely to be burned out and 53% less likely to consider leaving their company (McKinsey & Company and LeanIn. Org, 2021).

From personal experience of being the 'only' in many school and work environments, feeling that you have at least one person who is actively considering your experience makes such a huge difference – the difference between feeling like you're seen or totally invisible. I remember a time at one of my previous workplaces when my manager thought it would be a fun idea to play the 'guess the baby game'. This is when everyone anonymously submits a baby picture of themselves, after which the group will take turns to try and match a team member to each picture. Sounds like some lighthearted teambuilding fun, right? Who wouldn't want to look at funny pictures of their colleagues as babies? Except I was the only POC in the team. It, therefore, made no sense for me to play the game because I could be identified instantly. This didn't bother me to be honest – it's just a game. But it still didn't feel great that my manager had clearly failed to consider the respective identities present in the team, and how that would impact on equal engagement in the task.

I felt comfortable enough to call out this oversight, but it also felt great to have my point supported by some of my other colleagues who suggested other games we could play. This is a small, but effective, form of allyship that has stuck with me and is just one example of how we can use our privilege to better others. Before unpacking some more, it's useful to lay a solid foundation of what allyship is, and isn't, as there are several prominent misconceptions surrounding this work.

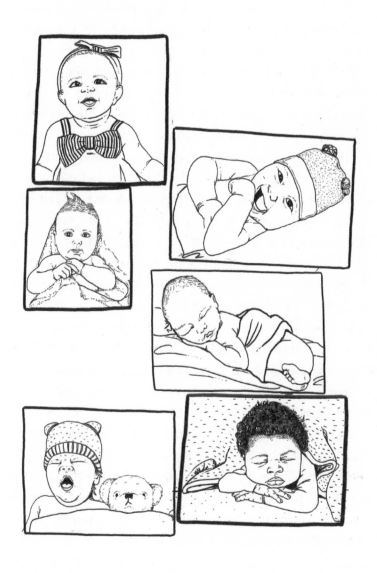

The first misconception is that, in order to be effective and impactful in your allyship, you need to have a full awareness and understanding of what being part of an oppressed group entails. Some claim that people from disadvantaged communities need to be understood first before they are advocated for. I commonly hear this in specific reference to the trans community, from well-meaning people who are cisgender. That they just 'don't get it', as they haven't experienced gender dysphoria before. Or haven't had a time in their lives thus far where they felt they might not identify with the gender they were assigned at birth. Some may also state their religious faith as a reason why they can't understand being trans, as it does not allow the possibility for such gender identities to exist. Therefore, while they are able to be respectful like they would be to all humans, they cannot extend their support. As a cis man, who was also raised as a strict Catholic, this is a sentiment I can empathise with, even if I can't relate. But consider this.

Imagine if you were walking down the street and spotted someone on the ground who appeared to be in considerable pain. They're rolling around in anguish and shouting that they tripped. Would your first reaction be to try to verify their claim, by looking around for confirmation of the object they tripped over? Maybe you would, so others couldn't trip over it too. But what if you couldn't find it? The pavement was completely clear with not a hazard in sight that you can identify. Would that stop you from helping the person up? Would this gap in your understanding hamper your ability to get the person medical attention? I'd guess that it wouldn't. It'd be helpful for sure! But not essential. Any knowledge you didn't have, you could potentially ask the person who fell, or even see if there were bystanders. Or you could focus on seeking medical authorities who would be best placed to give the person the care they need.

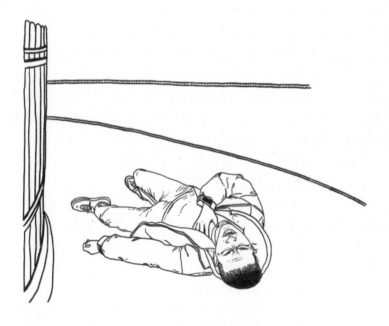

The point is that, while it's beneficial and ideal that we all understand each other intrinsically, it isn't an essential prerequisite to doing our best to be better to one another. Trans people deserve our understanding, compassion and validation. But most importantly, as a disadvantaged group, they need our support and advocacy. Respect is not enough and a lack of understanding is not a justifiable barrier. Arguably, we will all never truly understand what it is like to live each other's lives, so seeking this level of awareness is a futile task that can leave us frozen in a state of inaction that doesn't help anybody.

Another misconception is that allyship is about the person doing the work. This sounds a lot more obvious in theory than it can be in reality. Often when we think about helping others, we go into Batman mode. We see someone who needs our help as our bat signal in the sky, telling us to suit up and swoop in to save Gotham. However, do you notice how in the Batman movies (I haven't read the comics, so can't comment), we're rarely focused on the residents of Gotham? Despite the fact that Batman is meant to be saving the city from its latest threat, our focus is always on him and his exciting fight scenes with whoever his nemesis is on that occasion. Often Batman wins the dramatic final battle and drives off into the night, leaving the city in ruins. This is what happens when we just think about ourselves, and what we can do to potentially help others in a situation, rather than what is actually required.

In the context of racial justice, this can result in what is often described as 'White saviourism'. This is when White people think they have a superior ability to solve the issues People of Colour face, leading to harmful allyship attempts that are then performative and self-serving. A common example of this is groups of White people going to countries in Africa to dig wells and help out at orphanages. This is fine if the respective countries and their communities are in significant need of such aid. But unfortunately, they're often not – either because there are people from that country already doing that work who may just need financial support, education or training, and/or there are other issues that would benefit more from outsider assistance. Essentially, such groups often simply fail to ask how they can best help, or whether their efforts are required at all, resulting in ineffectual efforts that do more to benefit them (and their social media feeds) than the people they're meant to be helping. This saviourism can influence all forms of allyship, so it's important to be aware of. Being authentic allies requires us to decentre ourselves and our needs. Rather than being the main character, we need to choose to play a supportive role.

Studies on this subject indicate that disadvantaged communities favour allyship that prioritises building supportive relationships of trust over time, over seeking short-term recognition (Park et al, 2022). This is likely because allyship that predominantly serves the person doing the work is performative. That is to say, such actions are transactional and for show, rather than for the betterment of others. An example of this was 'Blackout Tuesday', an antiracism campaign that occurred on June 20th, 2020. The campaign was about everyone taking collective action to challenge racial injustice. Businesses and individuals alike were encouraged to pause their usual activities for a day and use the time to reflect on the impact of racism in their communities and what they could do to affect positive change.

To show solidarity and encourage others to join the

campaign, users of social media sites such as Instagram and Facebook started sharing black squares on their feeds, alongside the hashtag #BlackOutTuesday. Unfortunately, this is also where many people appeared to stop. While the intentions of posting a black square may be positive (I shared one myself), the act arguably became performative and redundant in impact when many didn't follow up with any action beyond the image. You can't and shouldn't take social media content as an accurate reflection of what actions people are taking offline. However, there was still a distinct lack of tangible follow-up acts after the squares were posted, which was disappointing to see. It felt like many simply wanted to signal that they were allies without doing the work of allyship.

Similarly, every Pride month, many organisations change their branding to represent the various LGBTQIA+ (lesbian, gay, bisexual, transgender, Queer/questioning, Intersex and Asexual) flags and even bring out Pride-themed merchandise. I love a Pride-themed shirt and believe awareness and solidarity are important advocacy tools. However, such acts arguably also become performative when organisations don't then take steps, within their means, to have a tangible positive impact on the LGBTQIA+ community.

All allyship should be conducted with a critical consideration of who the work is serving and the extent to which positive impact is being driven for the disadvantaged person or communities concerned – because allyship is also about action, not taking a static position. Arguably there is no such thing as being an ally, outside of the work of doing the work of allyship. To call yourself an ally almost implies that all of the work is done, or that you've done everything you can, when there is always someone who could use our assistance and support. It's also performative as it signals to others that you are someone who holds certain values, even if you don't act on them to benefit others. We, therefore, need to go beyond the ally label and think about how we can instead factor the work of allyship into our day-to-day. Because it's not enough to just be against prejudice and discrimination. By itself, this is not sufficient to influence the changes that so many need.

We should also think about the work of allyship as being something we do in small, intentional steps. Rather than broad strokes. One person can't fix the world's problems alone, it would be egotistical to think so, and ineffectual to try. We need to think about where we have the most power and influence in our lives to have the biggest impact and focus on showing up to do the work as consistently as we have the capacity to – because the work is not easy.

There are many reasons why systems of privilege and oppression persist, but a huge one is that people are often scared to step outside of their comfort zone on a consistent basis to work on challenging them. Because doing this is often uncomfortable. It requires having difficult conversations, breaking our normal routines and challenging the status quo. It involves accepting risks, and the possibility that you'll make mistakes. This is why we need to be motivated, but realistic. To try our best to do our bit, accept and act on feedback and never give up. Everybody – absolutely *everybody* – needs everyone to at least try.

Here are some practical, everyday ways that we can do this:

- *Educate yourself on experiences that you don't have.* As mentioned, you don't need to understand the exact ins and outs of what disadvantaged people and groups go through in order to support them. But it does help to increase your awareness of the challenges that others face. So, take the time to learn more about how the systems that advantage you work. Seek resources to inform yourself on pertinent social issues, and the role you can play to help address them. Most importantly, try your best to do this yourself, rather than demanding this information from disadvantaged groups. As the saying goes, Google is free, and just because someone holds a certain identity, doesn't mean that it's their job to educate you on their experience if they don't want to. Try to think outside the box too. Books are a great resource (of course) but there's so much you can learn by strategically following content creators and news sources on social media, or by diversifying your friendship circles.
- *Make an effort to listen to and validate the experiences of those around you.* As someone looking to play a supportive role, listening to the needs of whomever you're keen to support so you may therefore centre them is essential. Making an effort to tune into the experiences of those around you, will also heighten your awareness of disparities that you may have otherwise been unaware of, as they benefit you.

100

- *Use your wallet!* There's a hilarious content creator called Adam Martinez whose catchphrase is 'open your purse'. Clips of people saying the phrase go viral on my social feeds every few months, usually in response to a celebrity or public figure with perceived wealth expressing their thoughts and prayers in the wake of a crisis. As mentioned, there is a place for awareness and solidarity when it comes to social causes, and we also shouldn't make assumptions about what people are or aren't doing behind closed doors. However, it is undeniable that we live in a world where money is power. If you have the financial means to, for example, donate to charities, community projects and fundraisers, this is a powerful form of supportive allyship.

- *Make an effort to include those who find themselves excluded.* Whether that be someone who is excluded socially – for example, sitting by themselves at lunch – or excluded in a professional sense, for example, at work – a powerful form of allyship is to pass the mic to voices that are underrepresented whenever possible. If you are a cis man in a meeting with no gender diversity ask why. If asked to share a perspective on an experience you don't have, make an effort to bring in the opinion of someone who is of that experience. Use any power you may have to make space for those who have less than you.

- *While being mindful of your own safety and that of others, try to call out instances of injustice or unfair behaviour that you see occur.* Unfortunately, the ability to react authentically in every environment to such situations is a privilege that many don't have. For example, if you are one of only a few POC at work, you may feel less able to call out instances of racism that happen to you because you fear you won't be heard or understood. As a bystander, making the effort to call out such incidents, when they happen, is a powerful form of allyship, that not only potentially helps the target, but sets the tone for others that such behaviour is unacceptable. This can happen in both direct and indirect ways. For example, if someone makes a misogynistic joke, you could call it out, but you could also just refuse to laugh. It's important that we don't encourage prejudiced behaviour by condoning it.

- *Team up with, and support, those who are already doing the work to advocate for change.* Remember the Batman and Gotham analogy from earlier – sometimes when you effectively decentre yourself in your allyship, you can identify that there are already people doing the work that you are looking to do. There are already marginalised people, from all areas of society, who are challenging the injustices they face and could do with your support. So empower them. And encourage others to join you.

---

66 In the words of a wise woman called
Vanessa Amarosi, 'everybody needs everybody' 99

- *Be engaged.* The news cycle can be intense, but try your best to stay up to date, socially aware and engaged in local politics. When you have the opportunity, lobby and vote in favour of justice. Your voice matters.
- *Keep yourself accountable for your actions and commit yourself to supporting and uplifting those around you whenever you can.* It's not always easy, but in tough moments, ask yourself this question: if not you, then who? In the words of a wise woman called Vanessa Amarosi, 'everybody needs everybody'.

8

Why intersectionality and our uniqueness is important

Take it from me, being both Black and Queer is not for the faint of heart. Throughout my journey of self-discovery as a young teenager, these two parts of my identity always felt like they were at war within me. For a large portion of my youth, I believed that embracing my sexual orientation would mean that I'd have to betray and disown my racial identity. Because in my mind, you couldn't be both Black and Queer. The positive examples of being Queer and confident in the media, and the spaces I was in, were already limited, and the representation that did exist was almost solely of White people. The picture painted to me, by my community, of what a Black man should be like was also informed by fervent queerphobia and toxic masculinity. To be a Black man was to be strong, tall, tough and, most importantly, straight/cisgender. It felt like adhering to these standards was essential if I wanted to be a Black man in the 'right' way and be pro-Black. I always got the sense that to be anything different than the norm, whether that be the clothes I wore, the way I carried myself or the gender I fancied, was to deny my race and community. I had to be 'on-code'. Therefore, I never felt free to be authentically myself until I went to university.

Leaving my family home for university exposed me to a greater mix of people, and I was able to find Black and Queer communities who accepted and celebrated me in my most authentic form. Yet, like Natalie Imbruglia, I was still torn. My friends of colour couldn't completely relate to the homophobia I experienced, or why I wasn't always as comfortable as them in male-dominated Black spaces. My Queer circle was mostly White, so also couldn't fully relate to my experience as a Black man. How I was perceived differently to them by bouncers on nights out, or experienced racism on dating apps. Don't get me wrong, I was blessed to have found empathetic and understanding friends who I appreciate dearly to this day, but I was still in the position of having to explain myself. I only felt the true weight of this in hindsight, as an adult who is now blessed to have several Black Queer friends. Friends I don't have to unpack the nuances of my experience to, and with whom I always feel completely seen.

❝ Yet, like Natalie Imbruglia, I was still torn ❞

After a long journey of self-discovery, I now know that I am a Black, Queer, cis man with an awful singing voice, all at the same time. My identity is as nuanced as my experiences, and that doesn't take anything away from me or define who I am, but just how the world receives me in different contexts.

This is a truth that is not unique to me, or even to Black Queer people. We all have aspects of our identity that may impact the experiences we have in different environments. If you're a heavy metal superfan, this could be to your benefit while trying to make friends at a heavy metal gig. But maybe not if I invited you to one of my house parties, where the playlist is likely to involve a significant amount of Beyoncé. My friends may wonder why you don't know every syllable of 'Crazy in Love' and every move of the music video choreography, and then what? Well maybe you're also a single heterosexual man. As someone with lots of single heterosexual women as friends, this could possibly be to your advantage if you're down to mingle. But then consider if English isn't your first language. There could be a language barrier that hampers your flirt game. Or accentuates it. Who knows?

The point is that different parts of our identity provide us with certain advantages and disadvantages in certain environments. These can combine, overlap and intersect to produce unique experiences and obstacles for everybody. This means that, if you are part of a certain marginalised, or privileged group, it doesn't mean that you share the same issues, benefits or struggles as everyone else in that group. Not everyone who is Black experiences racism in the same way or has the same relationship with their Blackness.

That's because everyone is unique, which is a given, but also because Black people can be women and Queer and disabled, etc. All of these identity factors have their own influences on our experiences.

What I am describing here is the theory of intersectionality. This term was first coined and popularised by American law professor Kimberlé Crenshaw in her 1989 paper 'Demarginalizing the Intersection of Race and Sex'. The paper sees Crenshaw criticise the US justice system's use of single-category analysis at the time, which she felt disadvantaged people who exist at intersections of identity, specifically Black women. One case presented is that of a motor company that didn't hire Black women until 1964. They were forced to make seniority-based redundancies several years later, during which all of the Black women were let go. Some of the women sued the company for enacting a policy that unfairly targeted them as Black women. However, the court did not rule in their favour, as the company's policy had not been racist *or* sexist in nature. Which is true – it was both.

The theory of intersectionality highlights that we all hold multiple identities, which means that certain members of our communities are facing multiple forms of discrimination. Black women face both sexism and racism, and this should be considered when we think about being inclusive to members of this group. Being such an individual often means facing additional challenges and dealing with the stresses this entails. At the intersections of identity also lie unique challenges that we shouldn't ignore or erase.

This is why, when looking to be kinder to one another, and uplift and empower those who are marginalised, we need to keep intersectionality in mind. First and foremost, doing so reminds us that everyone is an individual, with unique experiences and needs, so therefore should be treated as such. When we fail to tailor the way that we show care to others, we are more likely to miss the mark, and potentially cause more harm than good. Failure to consider intersectionality can also result in us affirming structures of inequality that disadvantage certain identity groups, even if we are doing our best to deconstruct them.

An excellent example of this can be found when we look at women. Advocacy that looks to support all women should, in theory, consider all of the issues that those who identify as women face. However, this often does not work in practice, because among women, there are varying levels of power and privilege present. Arguably a cis White woman may benefit from access to more power than a trans, disabled Black woman. Even if this isn't the case, in specific instances there is a greater likelihood that, across the board, the experiences of the most privileged will rise to the top and be prioritised. Or that advocacy will benefit those who hold more power.

This is demonstrated by the approach to closing the gender pay gap in the UK. As I write, it is mandatory for companies to record and report on the gender pay gap between the men and women in their organisations. This data is vital for tracking the progress that is being made in addressing this issue. Yet ethnicity pay gap reporting is not mandatory in the UK. This means that, while we know that men in full-time work earn 7.9% more than women, it's unclear how women of colour fare within this percentage (Office for National Statistics, 2021). Arguably, an assumption is being made that all women are impacted by the same factors that drive gender pay disparities, and to the same extent. However, in the USA there is sufficient data to indicate otherwise. As just one example of how race and ethnicity can influence this pay disparity, while White women in the USA earn 79 cents for every dollar a White man earns, Black women only earn 62 cents (Bleiweis, 2020). This is a significant difference that highlights the specific struggles Black women may be facing in achieving equal pay. Struggles that would be largely ignored without an intersectional perspective being applied to the issue.

The same can also be said for the LGBTQIA+ community. Data indicates that members who are also of colour are more significantly impacted by discrimination in the workplace than their White counterparts. In the USA, a 2021 study found that a third of LGBTQIA+ People of Colour had experienced employment discrimination due to their sexual orientation/gender identity, compared to a quarter of White LGBTQIA+ people who said the same (School of Law Williams Institute, 2021). Also from personal experience, I have found that a lot of safe spaces that are meant to serve the whole community instead predominantly cater to cis gay White men. Or at least they don't make a sufficient effort to actively include and cater to all parts of the community. This is a key reason why UK Black Pride, founded in 2005, has hosted a sizable Pride event in London since 2018. There is a strong sentiment within the community that privilege affects who is seen and advocated for the most, and who has their experiences overshadowed in the mix.

This is why intersectionality is an effective and essential approach to inclusion. As it ensures that we are considering who may be left behind and tackling injustices from the root. It is in everyone's interest to dismantle all structures of oppression. If we allow ourselves to inadvertently prioritise the most privileged in our advocacy, these structures will still persist.

The theory of intersectionality also gives us a more comprehensive view of social issues, and their respective drivers. Unpacking issues in such a way provides the clarity required to truly understand why they occur. For example, data indicates that the COVID-19 pandemic had a disproportionate impact on POC in the UK, with all marginalised racial groups facing a higher risk of death from the virus than White people (British Medical Association, 2021). A non-intersectional view of this issue may potentially see this as being solely due to medical racism – and it is true that there is sufficient evidence to indicate that POC face racial bias in the UK health system – as seen in the disproportionately high numbers of women from this group who die in childbirth, discussed earlier. However, this is not the only driver, when it comes to exposure to COVID – another is arguably income status.

POC are proportionally more likely to live in low-income households and therefore are also more likely to be in low-paying roles that require them to be outside their home and exposed to the airborne virus (Social Metrics Commission, 2019). Of course, lack of access to different (or safer in this case) work opportunities as POC will also be influenced by racism. Therefore, making the consideration of intersectionality all so important when looking to tackle this issue among many others.

Sounds pretty clear, right? Most would agree, but this theory has been critiqued to the extent that it has a bad reputation in certain circles. While most of these critiques are misleading in my opinion, it's still important to unpack them in order to be best equipped to utilise this theory effectively.

The first common criticism is that it encourages a certain

'oppression Olympics' approach to discussions of privilege and marginalisation in society. The concern is that the discussion of the many disadvantaged identities one could hold, and how this affects experience, just results in a 'Top Trumps" effect (the card game where the person who holds a card that has the highest number in a certain category wins). This would place those who are deemed to have the most privilege as deserving of the least concern, and those who have racked up the most disadvantageous identities as deserving of the most concern. While I sympathise with the sentiment behind this (which is a fear that the needs of cis heterosexual White men will be disregarded entirely), I would argue that this criticism is rooted in a misunderstanding of how privilege and the theory of intersectionality actually work.

Having privilege, meaning that you benefit from an imbalance of power that results in unearned advantages, doesn't mean that you don't face any issues in life at all, as I discussed in the previous chapter on the topic. Likewise, having less privilege doesn't mean that you automatically live an awful life. There are many factors that can influence your trajectory besides privilege. However, if you are part of a privileged social group, this does mean that there are certain obstacles others face that you don't. So, when we are discussing dismantling structures of oppression and supporting oppressed people, those who aren't oppressed in a relevant way are naturally not of priority. This doesn't mean that they can't have issues that are worthy of attention and care, just that these are not driven by a certain structure of oppression, which we may be concerned about at a certain time. If you're a cis heterosexual White man and your dog sadly passes away, I'd hope that those around you would still be sympathetic regardless of your privileged identity.

> 66 There are no 'winners' or 'losers',
> only affected and unaffected parties 99

In inclusion there are no 'winners' or 'losers', only affected and unaffected parties. The theory of intersectionality is also about more than just affirming that multiple forms of discrimination can impact experience in an additive way. Black women, for example, don't just face double the discrimination for being part of these two groups, even though this may definitely expose them to more injustice. But they face unique issues that exist at the intersection of being Black and a woman, and this is what intersectionality calls us to acknowledge. There are no leagues when it comes to tackling injustice and, as mentioned, dismantling structures of oppression benefits us all.

There are also some who view the theory of intersectionality as cosigning a harmful, catch-all approach to inclusion. Essentially motivating people to focus more effort on covering all of the potential bases, rather than on having a meaningful positive impact. For example, companies that think a solution to a lack of diversity is to hire as many different 'types' of underrepresented employees as possible, without considering whether their workplace is inclusive and accommodating of such individuals so they may thrive. This is a valid concern. Any ambitions one may have to only appear to be super inclusive are inherently self-serving and performative. But I would again argue that this isn't what the theory of intersectionality is about. We do need to acknowledge the breadth of the unique challenges faced by those who hold intersectionally marginalised identities. However, addressing these challenges still requires tailored, intentional action. If anything, the theory of intersectionality should encourage us to be as specific and tailored as possible in our approach to inclusion, allyship and challenging injustices.

Finally, intersectional perspectives are accused by some of deliberately attempting to make those with the most privilege in society feel bad and guilty for who they are. Which seems unfair, as no one chooses to be the identity that they are. To quote Lady Gaga, we are indeed all just born this way. To this, I would say that it is completely normal to feel uncomfortable when discussions of privilege and intersectionality are being had. It forces us all, even those who are marginalised in some way, to confront the fact that there are many unique struggles that so many people face that we don't even think about. I will truly never understand what it is like to be a trans individual in our current society or all of the ways that I benefit from being cis. However, focusing on guilt is not helpful and, therefore, ultimately, not aligned with the true purpose of intersectionality as a theory. The aim is to help illuminate intersectional struggles

117

and privileges so we can work towards creating a society that is more equal for everyone. It's not taking something from someone more privileged and giving it to someone less so, it's about sharing the opportunities in a mindset of abundance. The theory has a purpose that goes way beyond desiring to get us in our feelings.

> 66 To quote Lady Gaga, we are indeed all just born this way 99

Our emotions are valid, but we need to push through any discomfort in order to focus on the work that needs to be done to achieve positive change for those who need it most. To help you get started, here are a few practical ways that you can use the theory of intersectionality to have a positive impact on those around you:

- *Always keep intersectionality in mind when celebrating periods in the calendar that are dedicated to driving awareness.* Like Pride month, Black History Month and Mental Health Awareness Week. Try to dig deep and consider the various intersections that may be present within the respective group that is being focused on, and how you can use the opportunity to ensure that everyone is seen and heard. If you are a manager, think about how certain activities or practices you have might favour some over others and adjust accordingly.

118

- *Consider the privilege you hold and how you can make room for the people who exist at the intersections of the communities you are a part of that may be underrepresented.* For example, if you are a White cis gay man that is part of a Pride network or an LGBTQIA+ focused workplace or community group, critically consider whether all parts of the community are represented in what your group does. Think of the Queer safe spaces you attend, and whether they are safe for all members of the LGBTQIA+ community. Those who may be of colour, trans, disabled. If not, how can this be changed?
- *Don't have a generalised idea of how you think someone may react to, or be affected by an issue, based on what you assume their identity is.* Intersectionality highlights that there is not a singular shared experience within communities, and you can't assume to know all parts of someone's identity just by looking at them.
- *Remember to not oversimplify terminology in a way that may be exclusionary.* For example, when discussing issues related to abortion and menstruation, remember that this doesn't just impact cis women, but also trans individuals. So, it's important to use trans-inclusive language, such as 'people with uteruses' or 'those with the capacity to get pregnant'. Doing this doesn't take away from the needs of dominant groups, but just brings people who exist at intersections that are often overlooked into the conversation. These are also often people who need our focus the most.
- *If you hold a marginalised identity, seek opportunities to*

collaborate and invest in the efforts that other groups are making to achieve equality and justice. Not only is injustice everyone's issue, but intersectionality highlights that doing so will only serve to benefit your community too. For example, anti-racist efforts should go hand-in-hand with feminist efforts, and anti-ableism efforts, and so on. Teamwork really makes the dream work.

9

Why equity is better than equality

Something that many lovely, well-meaning White people have said to me in the past is that they don't see colour. That someone could be white, black, red, green or blue for all they care, as they treat everyone as an individual. This *should* be the ultimate goal. We are, indeed, all individuals, and while our identities influence our experiences and how the world receives us, they don't define who we are as people. I am much more than my race, my sexual orientation, gender and so on.

So then why does this idea – people not seeing colour, or being 'colour blind' – make me and not just me, many others, feel so uncomfortable?

Because, while the intent of this phrase may be a positive one, informed by idealistic ambitions for an equal society, the impact falls flat.

As much as I would love to be able to look past race in my everyday life, the current state of the world that we live in doesn't make this possible. For example, as a Black person in the UK, I am nine times more likely to be stopped and searched by the police, under suspicion of criminal activity (GOV.UK, 2020). This doesn't define who I am as a person, but it is something I am consciously aware of when I pass police officers while walking through the streets of London.

People of Colour aren't often afforded the luxury of being able to see themselves outside of the lens of race. The ability to do this is a form of privilege – it's the power afforded to those who are perceived as the default. If you can remove the influence of race from the interactions you have with others, this is a sign that you benefit from a sense of individualism. POC often have to manage facing judgement that's based on the assumptions others have about their race. All of this makes the statement 'I don't see colour' more of an insensitive claim than is likely intended. Its use signifies a lack of awareness.

We need to be aware of race and 'see' colour in order to challenge racial injustice. If you don't see my race, you're also not seeing the challenges I face, or acknowledging the experiences that I, and those who look like me, have. As mentioned, I do believe that most people who say they don't see colour are well-intentioned, and most likely are people who engage in anti-racist allyship or, at least, don't have racist beliefs. However, perpetuating the idea of race-neutrality actually has a harmful, counterintuitive impact on People of Colour. Because it creates environments where conversations regarding race and racism can't thrive. Where POC don't feel as comfortable to be honest about their experiences, because in such spaces, race 'is not a thing'.

This stifles and hampers productive conversations and suppresses voices that are already struggling to be heard.

This is why saying that 'all lives matter' in response to the statement that Black lives matter, is so harmful. Yes, all lives do matter. However, the purpose of saying that *Black* lives matter is to specifically highlight that Black people often face situations where their lives are devalued. The discussion of *all* lives mattering rings hollow when you're aware that the lives of so many clearly matter a lot less. It has an impact that is dismissive.

Saying that you don't see colour, as a White person, is also a way of centring yourself in your allyship to POC. It carries the connotation that racism isn't your issue or problem anymore, as you have done the work. You are one of the good ones, so are entitled to disengage. This is inherently performative, as it has little to no positive impact on anyone but the individual in question. Doing this is similar to calling yourself an ally without doing any work. Dismantling the systems that privilege White people at the expense of POC requires that White people be aware of the unearned advantages they have. So that they can do their bit to try and correct racial power imbalances, and also to enable the making of racially sensitive decisions.

It also just doesn't feel great to think that you need to assimilate in order to be seen as being of equal value and worth. Saying that you would rather not see me as a Black person is not the compliment you may think it is. It actually feels like erasure. We are all different from one another, whether it be by definition of race, gender, sexual orientation or another attribute relating to our identity or background. Inclusion should be a celebration of difference, not a blindness to it. Advocating for assimilation before equality is achieved also, conveniently, overlooks the challenges that marginalised communities face in a false pursuit of progress. It deflects the sole responsibility of solving social issues to the people faced by such issues when we all need to be doing our part to contribute towards equality.

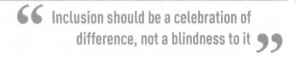

Inclusion should be a celebration of difference, not a blindness to it

To do this, we need to be in pursuit of equity, rather than equality. Equity and equality are often seen as the same and, in many ways, they are both sides of the same coin. However, they lead to different outcomes. Equality is when you give everyone the same amount of resources and treat everybody the same, regardless of who they are and what they need. Treating everyone with a sense of equality is the belief behind aspiring not to see race. While equity is when you make a needs assessment before deciding how to treat others and allocate resources. The aim of equality is to act in a fair way, the aim of equity is to try to achieve a fair outcome. So, in the context of race, equity means acknowledging that marginalised racial groups lack certain race-based advantages that White people have. This means that they need to be treated differently to enable the fairest outcome for such groups.

Arguably, equity is the most direct route to achieving fairness and correcting inequalities, while equality maintains and can actually worsen inequalities. Which is something that sounds like it shouldn't make sense. To say that it's fair to treat everyone differently feels somewhat contradictory. But this image, by Angus Maguire, illustrates how this works in a helpful way.

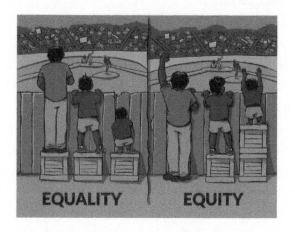

On the left is what equality looks like, i.e. treating everybody the same. Equality says that the three people who are trying to watch the game from over the fence should be given one box to stand on. Despite the fact that they are of varying heights. The result is that the tallest person has a great view of what's happening, the slightly shorter person has an adequate view, and the shortest person can't see at all. This is the fairest approach to the distribution of the boxes. But it actually results in an unfair outcome when the needs of the group are taken into consideration. However, the image on the right is an equity approach to the distribution of the boxes, which is arguably unfair. In this version, the tallest person is judged not to need a box to stand on at all. Instead, their box is given to the shortest person, who now has the most boxes of all. But now everyone in the group has exactly the same view. The unfair approach to box distribution has actually resulted in the fairest outcome.

Equity is an optimum approach to achieving fairness and equality because it's proportionate in nature. Which means that when we apply an equity approach to addressing challenges, all needs are met to the extent that they're required, if there is sufficient capacity.

For example, consider if you are the headmaster of a school. It's necessary for there to be a set minimum standard for all of the teachers to get their students to meet, and hopefully exceed. However, due to students inevitably having varying levels of capability with each subject in the curriculum, attention should ideally be divided equitably. More attention and focus should be placed on supporting students in areas where they struggle, with less provided on subjects they excel in. When applied across the board, this should allow each student a similar opportunity to thrive in their studies.

But what about the students that are bright and excel in all areas? Why are they being punished for being successful?

The extremely capable students are not being punished,

or unjustly treated by receiving less attention. The resources allocated to such students don't reflect their value, worth or how we feel about them as individuals, but rather the fact that there are many factors that mean that they are already ahead. This could be something as inherent as natural intellect. Or it could be that they have access to home tutoring, trips abroad to experience different cultures, a spacious and quiet home to study in or the freedom of not having a family member that's dependent on them for care. Whatever it is, they are a few steps ahead already. And resources in almost all school environments are limited – if not by money, then by time.

Providing those who require more assistance with additional support, while ensuring that everyone has what they need to achieve a minimum standard, doesn't punish anyone. It actually ensures that everyone is rewarded with a fair shot at excelling and being their best with the resources that are available. Choosing to split resources equally just increases the chances that some will be left behind.

Equity is the key to addressing many social injustices that the world faces, for example, the significant gender pay gap between men and women in the UK and USA (and beyond). Closing the gap requires that particular attention be given to the salaries awarded to women across industries, and the progression opportunities they are afforded. Depending on the context, this assessment may expose the need for equitable solutions, such as targeted pay increases and progression schemes, to bolster the potential that women have to achieve parity of income with men.

Like the school example, such measures, if required, are not a reflection of anyone's inherent value or worth. They don't imply that women are less capable, or that men deserve to be mistreated in some way because of their gender. They just acknowledge that the playing field is not level, and extra effort is required to allow everyone an equal opportunity to earn and progress, in relation to their ability and experience.

On the topic of wealth and income, closing the significant wealth gap in the UK arguably also requires an equity approach to support the most vulnerable. Data indicates that the majority of households in the UK that are living in relative poverty are White households – specifically 76%, which is huge (Social Metrics Commision, 2019). However, the poverty rate among White households is actually the lowest, a mere 19%, compared to 46% of Black households and 37% of Asian households (Social Metrics Commision, 2019). It could be said that this issue requires an equality approach, where all low-income households are supported the same. However, this arguably ignores the fact that there are drivers present that make households that are a certain race more susceptible to being of a low-income. An intersectional analysis is also likely to highlight additional obstacles affecting all low-income racial groups. An equitable approach would therefore be more effective in achieving equality in this area by providing targeted, tailored support as part of wider efforts to narrow the gap for all.

Choosing equity over equality can arguably raise additional obstacles, however, that are important to consider.

It firstly implies that there is always a consensus on the extent to which different needs should be met, which is, more often than not, the opposite of the case. Individuals are likely to hold different opinions on what they consider to be a fair and just outcome, meaning that equitable decisions are more likely to be challenged. As opposed to equality decisions, which are objective in nature, everything is split as equally as possible. This can result in opposition and critique that are tough to handle. However, it is also necessary, as equitable decisions can also hamper fair outcomes if they are not explained and defended adequately. Decisions on resource allocation based on needs that aren't clarified is favouritism that can hide biased decisions. Transparency is an essential part of equitable efforts.

Related to this, equitable decisions should be based on data not assumptions, otherwise our focus and energies may be misplaced, resulting in those who need help falling through the cracks and ultimately ending up worse off. An interpersonal example of this can be found in friendships. It's common to have some friends who require more support than others. Some of our loved ones may face more obstacles and have experienced more hardship than others. People also have different temperaments and personalities – some people like to share and talk through their experiences, while others like to just get on with things. It's fine and reasonable to have unique relationships with the people in your life and cater to their needs accordingly. However, we should also be careful not to make assumptions about the needs of our 'strong friends'. Those who may be less likely to reach out or generally tend not to need our support. Even if someone generally tends to be fine, it's still kind to check-in on occasion to ensure that this is indeed the case. Many people who appear to be strong are suffering in silence, and they may continue to do so if we make assumptions about their state without checking. One in four UK adults who experience significant mental health issues that affect their day-to-day say that they would wait more than six months to seek care, or never seek care at all (Surgo Ventures, 2021). So always base equitable decisions on evidence.

Finally, it's important to remember that while equity is required to enable fair outcomes and achieve equality, this is not the end, or at least it shouldn't be. Once we have made efforts to level the playing field, justice should be the ultimate goal. Think back to the Angus Maguire drawing of the people looking over the fence (see page 127). In the short term, the equitable distribution of boxes is essential for enabling a fair outcome so everyone has the same opportunity to watch the game. However, once this happens, or even while this is happening, we should also be thinking about what changes can be made to stop this from being an issue in the future. Does the fence need to be there? Could we work with the stadium organisers to take it down? Or liaise with the three people to secure them a better vantage point for the next game? That is what justice looks like – assessing what leads to unfair outcomes for some over others and eliminating these causes. For some challenges, like the fence, this is achievable in the short term. For others, such as systemic oppression, this is a long-term struggle that is bigger than all of us. But this should always be our North Star. Equity is an essential first step, so we are supporting those who need our help the most today. But all efforts should also be contributing towards a future where everyone has similar access to resources, opportunities and fair outcomes in life.

If you are looking to promote equity in your everyday, these are two practical things you can do:

1. *Consider differences in outcomes within your environments, whether that be at school, work or in your community.* Does everyone have the same chances? Do the policies that govern your spaces advantage or disadvantage some more than others? If there are disparities in outcomes, consider what is driving these, and what can be done to challenge them. This could be as simple as critically considering your work social calendar. Does your organisation put on social events that cater to a wide range of interests and requirements? Or are they all trips to the pub late on a Thursday night? There is nothing wrong with a company paying for their employees to go to the pub – I myself am partial to such a trip. But if these are the only socials that are being provided, then the company is likely not meeting the social needs and requirements of its workforce, even though it may appear that they are making an effort to. Not everyone drinks alcohol and feels comfortable in drinking establishments. It's also possible that some employees may

have young families, so can't always hang out late at night after work. An equitable decision would be to ensure that, of the socials that are run, at least some are ones that cater to the needs and interests of those who can't or don't want to go to the pub. So that everyone can feel like they are part of the organisation. As a member of the organisation, this is a point you could raise, whether you are part of the affected group or not, to contribute towards equity. Remember that advocacy and allyship don't have to be about broad strokes but are also effective in small intentional acts.

2. *Help others understand the importance of equity*. A significant hindrance to attempts to strive for equity over equality is a lack of understanding. This is understandable, as it goes against the commonly promoted belief that our society is meritocratic, and that equality is the fairest approach to have. Additionally, as mentioned, equitable acts that lack transparency have the potential to be perceived as unjustified favouritism and bias. So one way we can all enable efforts towards achieving equity to thrive, if we have the capacity to, is to inform others of its importance, and why it's the optimum route to achieving fairness.

10

Why we shouldn't 'other', objectify or stereotype people

We all share a common desire to belong. It's human to seek this out from our family, friends, the spaces we like to socialise in and the environments we work in. Most would agree that feeling like you're out of place, or unwelcome, is very uncomfortable. It is true that we can sometimes intentionally put ourselves in such situations to discover new things about ourselves or have beneficial developmental experiences. For example, deciding to finally commit to taking that solo trip or attend a house party by yourself. Moments of discomfort such as these are beneficial for our growth and it's important to push ourselves when possible. But there is an undeniable pleasure to be found in the comfort of knowing that you are right where you are meant to be. It's similar to pulling on a well-worn pair of warm comfy socks on a chilly evening. To me, this is what it means to feel at home. Home isn't necessarily the house you were raised in or even necessarily a physical place. But simply anywhere we feel like we belong and can be our most authentic selves.

We all also have the capacity to make others feel like they don't belong with our words and our actions. That there's something about them that sets them apart and doesn't make them one of *us*. There are many intentional and overt ways to do this, like crossing the road when you see someone, not inviting someone to your birthday party or even verbally expressing hate towards a certain person or group. As people who are consciously trying to be as kind as we can to others, these are things we may already be aware of. But we also need to be aware of the unintentional and covert ways that we can exclude others in our everyday lives, despite the fact that we don't mean to. Being aware of the small, unconscious exclusionary habits we may have just helps create environments that are as nurturing for others as we would want for ourselves so we can all feel at home.

One consideration that is important is what questions we choose to ask when we're getting to know new people. For example, 'where are you from?' This is probably the most common question to ask of anyone you're not familiar with. It usually comes from a place of genuine curiosity and interest, as well as a desire to establish common ground. Plus, it's just a basic element of small talk, along with asking how many siblings someone has and what they plan to have for dinner. You say this as a way to make conversation and be friendly.

The impact of this question does very much depend on who you are asking, however – and the context you are asking in. For example, consider the impact of this question if it is posed to someone who is very obviously different from those around them. Maybe you've asked this of someone at a bar, and they are the only person that is of a certain race there. Or they don't have the same accent as everyone else. Therefore this is someone likely already to be distinctly aware of their own difference. In such a situation, posing the 'where are you from?' question, could feel like the enquirer is looking to highlight this difference, which could be taken in a positive or negative way. This could be a positive thing for the object of the question if they are maybe on holiday. If I am abroad on vacation, being asked where I'm from is a potential opportunity for cultural exchange. In fact, I anticipate having to answer this question, as I've intentionally placed myself in the position of the outsider, in taking a short trip abroad.

Then also consider if you're asking this question to someone who is very obviously different at a bar, but this time it is a work social and everyone there is from the same company. In such a context, it could seem like you are high-lighting that person's difference in a negative way. Maybe to imply that they don't belong as much as everyone else at the company, because of their race or accent. The impact of this may also be exacerbated when the first answer is not accepted by the person asking, and a follow-up of 'where are you *really* from?' is offered. As a Black British person, this question and follow-up is something I have faced often in my hometown of London. In such a scenario, I am able to read between the lines and gather that they are likely curious about my ethnicity. However, the question still carries the assumption that I can't really be from London and the UK because of the colour of my skin. It is a question still too often asked of POCs.

This is something that's important to be aware of, as the experience of being in an underrepresented group in environments like the workplace can already be an isolating one. Such questions have the potential to worsen this feeling and make people feel like they are being singled out and judged because of who they are.

Directing such enquiring questions towards people who may hold identities or have backgrounds that are different to the majority can also force them into a box of limiting assumptions. For example, in the past, I've been asked if I'm familiar with (*insert the name of a Ghanaian person*

140

somebody went to school with or lived next door to once here). Or whether I enjoy jollof rice or am always late (two things that are synonymous with Ghanaian/West African culture). These questions are often well-intentioned, however, it does feel like I am immediately being classified. These types of questions can pressure people to feel like they have to become a representative of their cultural background. While I am proud of my ethnicity, it's not something I always want to unpack with people I don't know very well, especially if I am in a homogenous environment where I already stick out as being different. Have you considered that maybe I just want to blend in and get on with it?

This is an experience that you are less likely to have if you are, for example, White in a predominantly White country, like the UK, or if your accent is the same as the one common to your area. This is because being part of a dominant group affords you the privilege of being the default. You are unlikely to be made to feel like you don't belong because you share a common identity with the majority of those around you. Being part of a privileged group means that you aren't as impacted by certain assumptions and stereotypes about who you are. For example, a White person born and raised in Wales but now living in England may feel more open to discussing their heritage at work than a British South Asian woman born and raised in London. Because despite the South Asian woman arguably being more aligned with English culture than the Welsh person, their race denies them the

141

power of 'normal'. They are already on the back foot with regard to fitting in.

'Where are you really from?' is just one of many micro-aggressions that are faced by people who hold marginalised social identities. Microaggressions are subtle, indirect and sometimes unintentional forms of discrimination. The term was coined by American psychiatrist Chester M Pierce in the 1960s, initially to describe the many ways that Black people were put down, in their interactions with White people. However, since the term was coined, its impact has been demonstrated to go beyond racism. Microaggressions essentially just imply that the target isn't valued and doesn't belong. For example, expressing incredulous surprise at how well someone speaks, by saying 'Wow, you're so articulate! This statement implies that the person in question shouldn't be as capable to express themselves because of who they are. Such a comment is arguably fairly harmless in isolation and could be brushed off without major issue. However microaggressions are a powerful discriminatory force when in multitude.

A popular analogy that is used to demonstrate this is that of bee stings. Getting stung once or twice by a bee is annoying, but not a major issue for most – you'll feel uncomfortable for a few days and experience swelling, but that's it. Now imagine if you were stung by a bee every day for a month. This would probably become a more pressing issue in your life. Now imagine being stung by several bees, every day for a year. Such an assault would have a significant negative impact on your quality of life. Microaggressions

oppress in the same way. Because they are rooted in biases that people have about others, and members of marginalised groups face significant negative biases in society, they often bear the continuous brunt of microaggressions. This looks like consistently having your capacity to speak in an articulate way be challenged because you may have a certain accent. For example, data indicates that in the UK, people with distinct minority ethnic accents, or accents stereotypically associated with low-income communities in industrial towns, such as those from Birmingham and Liverpool, are judged as sounding less professional (Queen Mary University of London & the University of York, 2020). This can have a knock-on impact, affecting access to job opportunities, and levels of self-confidence. Indeed, studies show that microaggressions are a contributing factor to declining physical and mental health (Nadal, 2018).

Microaggressions are also 'othering' in nature, in a way that can have a distinctly negative impact on the life outcomes of people who hold certain social identities. To understand what it means to other somebody, look no further than the classic movie *Mean Girls* (2004). The lunch table, where popular girls Regina, Karen and Gretchen sit, is a manifestation of the power that the girls hold over the school. To be accepted on to their table is to share in their power as a member of the in-crowd, and being on the table requires an adherence to certain rules and standards. Anyone who isn't sat at the table is automatically of a lesser social standing, a member of the out-crowd. They do not fit in with the rules and standards that are required of those sitting at the table, and are considered lesser because of it. This is why it is so devastating for the head popular girl Regina George when she experiences some weight gain and is forced to wear sweatpants on a Monday (the horror!). It subsequently means she has to forfeit her place at the table.

Othering works in the same way – people are categorised as being different from a certain desirable group, which is then used as a justification to lower their social value in comparison. This usually works across a power dynamic that favours those who hold power and privilege, as, similar to the popular girls in *Mean Girls*, they have the ability and influence required to decide the rules. So, for example, White people, cis men and people of high income are not as easily othered by those who are more limited in regard to power and voice, say, Black people, trans people and those of low income. This can lead to sinister outcomes, as when members of certain groups are devalued and dehumanised, this can be used to justify discrimination and hate crimes. Othering also allows prejudices to persist, as stripping members of certain groups of their humanity can also cause us to have less empathy for them because we don't see ourselves in them. Anything that others, like microaggressions, is therefore a contributor towards societal oppression, and something we should all be wary of in our own actions and be prepared to call out in the actions of others.

One way othering can also occur is through language – such as coded language. These are words and phrases that are so often used in association with certain groups of people, that members of such groups become synonymous with the meaning of the word/phrase. For example, the word 'thug'. This is a word that's often used in the media and popular culture in association with reports and fictional depictions of Black people. To the extent that the word thug is now considered by many to be racially charged, despite its dictionary definition being race-neutral. This has a devaluing impact on Black people in society, who are more readily associated with harmful behaviour than their counterparts.

Another example is the way that news stories are reported. Look at this now infamous 2005 piece by the Associated Press following the tragedy of Hurricane Katrina in New Orleans. The same thing is happening in both photos – the survivors are taking provisions from a grocery store. Yet the Black person is described as 'looting', while the White people are 'finding'. The words 'finding' and 'looting' have distinctly different connotations, and describing the Black person in a negative light for doing the same thing is to position them as inherently different, and less favourable. Decisions like these, unintentional or otherwise, have an othering impact that can cause significant harm for the target groups. It's therefore important to make an active choice to challenge social norms and be as inclusive as possible in our actions.

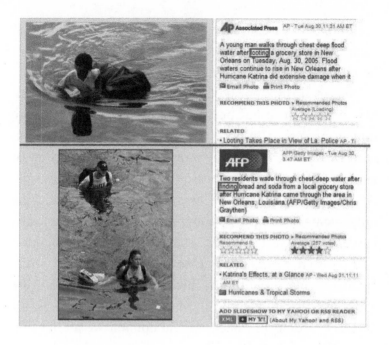

So, in the context of wanting to know where someone you just met is from, making a conscious effort to not have an othering impact looks like critically considering whether asking 'where are you from?' – or worse, 'where are you *really* from?' – is the best approach. It may be more sensitive to have this information come up organically as you get to know the person, rather than asking such a direct question, especially if you notice an obvious difference in who they are compared to everyone else. People are usually quite open to sharing more about themselves if given the space and comfort to do so, on their own terms. If there is an important reason why you need to ask for this information directly, it is always best to be transparent, and just ask what

147

their ethnicity is or where they grew up. This will make it clear what you mean, and there is no ambiguity that could be cloaking harmful assumptions.

We can also try our best not to objectify based on identity. So, try not to put people who hold identities that are underrepresented in a certain environment in a position where they feel they have to represent an entire group or fit into limiting perceptions or stereotypes about people who share their identity. This can be done by not making judgemental assumptions about how intelligent people are, based on their accents. Or asking people for the opinion that their group has on an issue – as a Black person, while I can provide insights into how racism impacts my life and ways that this could be mitigated, I can't speak for all Black people, or vouch for the opinion we all have on things. Remember that unless I am being paid to do so, it is also not my job or duty to educate you. To believe that any of the aforementioned is true is to objectify me based on my race.

We also need to be wary and conscious of reinforcing positive stereotypes that also serve to objectify members of certain groups. All stereotypes, bad or good, support the idea that we can hold certain beliefs, or assign certain characteristics to people, based on their identity. Which is harmful, either way. For example, there is a prominent stereotype that Black people are physically stronger and tougher than other races, with people citing Black men's dominance of sports like athletics and basketball as evidence of this. However, whether it is true or not that Black people have the potential to be stronger and faster, it is nonsensical to assume that the average Black person who is not an athlete must therefore be strong and tough.

Research indicates that young Black men are perceived to be stronger than young White men among non-Black people (Hugenberg & Rule, 2017). This assumption results in pressures being placed on young Black boys to automatically be better at sports, even when they have no natural ability or desire to be. Additionally, such beliefs about Black people can feed into their perceived threat in the eyes of law enforcement and contribute to healthcare bias. Studies indicate that, in the USA, Black and African American patients are 22% less likely than White ones to be prescribed pain medication (Sabin & Greenwald, 2012).

There are many other perceived positive stereotypes that we should take care to not reinforce. For example, the stereotype that all women have a maternal instinct or are more loving and nurturing than men. This places objectifying gendered expectations on women and can also contribute to an unequal distribution of labour in the home. Or the stereotype that all gay men are cis, physically fit, fashionable and every cis woman's best friend. This is another incredibly objectifying stereotype that denies gay people the capacity to be themselves. It can also lead to feelings of inadequacy if you are, for example, a gay man who is not physically fit. Body image issues within this community are rife, with many risking their lives through heavy steroid use and restrictive diets to try and look a certain way. It can also be incredibly hurtful to be labelled as the 'gay best friend'. While this is a common trope for a reason, it's objectifying and othering to have the value and worth of an important intimate relationship reduced to just your sexual orientation.

There are many practical ways that we can avoid unintentionally objectifying, stereotyping and othering those around us. One is to always be conscious of the position of power and privilege that we hold in relation to others. To always consider critically how the impact of the things we say or the actions we take may be influenced by someone's identity and background. Make an effort to see things from other people's perspectives and through the lens of other people's experiences. We can also do our best to disbelieve, challenge and work to dismantle any stereotypical narratives concerning those who are different from us, while leaning away from, rather than into, the assumptions we hold, to ensure that we're giving everyone the chance to be their own person. It also helps to try and nurture an authentic interest in the lives of others. Because when we know and understand each other better, it's easier for us to do right by one another.

11

How to apologise

For a case study on how *not* to apologise, look no further than Justin Timberlake. Let me set the scene. The year was 2004, and Janet Jackon and Justin Timberlake were performers at the iconic Super Bowl Halftime Show, alongside a handful of noughties music stars, including Nelly and P Diddy. After an electrifying set that was broadcast live to millions, Justin and Janet united for an incredibly suggestive duet of Justin's hit 'Rock Your Body'. At the song's ending line, 'bet I'll have you naked by the end of this song', Justin reached over and pulled away a portion of Janet's costume, exposing her uncovered breast for a split second.

The incident set the USA, and the world, aflame. What happened was quite clearly an accident – while the move was orchestrated, by the look of shock on both of their faces, it was obvious that Justin had accidentally torn off more of the costume than intended. However, it was still considered unacceptable indecent exposure by many, with the network receiving half a million complaints from viewers in the US. It also made headlines around the world, and the video is one of the most viewed and shared clips in history.

Despite the fact that both artists were equally involved in the scandal, and arguably Justin was the one who caused the incident by pulling away too much material, the consequences were starkly different for each party. Justin Timberlake's career didn't suffer, in fact, it took off, and he was able to move on to earn Grammys, increased radio play and chart success. Janet Jackson on the other hand was widely blamed for the mishap, with many alleging that she orchestrated the malfunction deliberately. She was made to apologise, lost several sponsorships and had her music videos and singles banned from rotation across all channels for months. Janet was also widely disparaged in the press for years, and the incident turned into a joke. Many would argue that her career has never been the same since – in terms of sales and chart success, it hasn't at all.

This is arguably a representation of the misogyny present within the media and entertainment industries, and the differences in how women's and men's bodies are perceived. Justin also failed to use his privileged position to defend Janet from the backlash or take accountability for the part he played in the scandal. He instead proceeded to leave Janet out to dry. A statement he released post-incident had no mention of Janet and merely stated that he was sorry if people were offended. For many years afterwards, Justin brushed the incident off as not being that serious, a minor, unintentional accident. As the years went on, he appeared to grow to accept that he didn't get as much of the blame as he should have and that he could have handled things better, but still gave no specific mention of how Janet had been treated, and the part he played in the situation.

It would take until 2021 for Justin to provide Janet with a direct apology, within the caption of a post on Instagram. The statement mentioned her by name and acknowledged that he had failed her. Sadly, in the same post he also partially justified his actions, claiming that he was ignorant at the time. He also did not specifically clarify what exactly he was apologising for. As far as taking accountability goes, to say that Justin fell short is an understatement.

The ability to apologise is an important skill to have. When our actions result in somebody else being negatively affected, an apology cannot reverse the harm, but it provides validation for, and recognition of, the victim's feelings and experiences. It is the least we can do to acknowledge that we have done wrong, or not acted in the best way, whether our actions were intentional or otherwise. Choosing not to provide the people we harm with this acknowledgement can have a significant impact on their self-esteem and self-worth. Owning up to the consequences of our actions is an impactful act of kindness towards others. Apologies also indicate to the people we're around that we respect their needs and boundaries and understand how they deserve to be treated. Giving apologies can bring us closer to one another and build trust or restore trust when it has been lost.

Having a willingness to apologise is also something that only serves to benefit us as people. When we take accountability for wrongdoing, we are also acknowledging our own humanity. We are all imperfect beings, and no one's life is devoid of mistakes. When we make apologies an everyday part of our lives, we allow ourselves the freedom to be authentically ourselves and accept all of our shortcomings. The liberating impact that this has also empowers us to make decisions in the pursuit of kindness and justice. The fear of making mistakes can often freeze us in a state of indecision that is ultimately detrimental. When we let go of perfection, we're able to make better choices, rather than safe ones. Apologising also forces us to acknowledge our mistakes, which in turn provides us with the opportunity to learn from them. A phrase I love is 'when you know better, you do better', and apologies are a great way to develop our self-awareness over time, so we can be kinder and more sensitive to others.

When you know better, you do better

However, I would also argue that if we apologise unnecessarily this does more harm than good, for us and any involved parties. As a Brit, this is something that's very close to home. Research indicates that British people say sorry fifteen times for every time an American does (YouGov, 2015). British politeness is a renowned phenomenon, and as apologisers go, we are world-class athletes. I've apologised to inanimate objects before, just for being in their way. It may seem like a good thing to always be prepped and ready to say sorry. However, when taken to far too great an extent, we risk getting into bad habits, like apologising for who we are, for the needs we have.

This can happen in small ways that have a significant impact over time, like saying sorry before stating your opinion in a work meeting. Though this could be seen by some as a polite way to interject into a conversation, more often it is you apologising for offering your opinion and excusing how you feel when it is your right (and job) to do so. This can have a significant impact on your confidence over time. No matter what the environment is, our needs and voices have inherent value and we all have an equal right to be heard and feel listened to. The impact of over apologising this way also disproportionately impacts those who are already othered within society and forced to speak louder to be heard. For example, in the UK and US, women are significantly more likely to apologise than men (YouGov, 2015).

We also should be careful not to apologise just to appease our own guilt, with no concern for the impact that our apology may have on the affected person. Taking account-ability for harm caused shouldn't cause further harm. For example, insisting that you speak to someone to apologise is counterintuitive if they have explicitly requested that they have no contact with you. In such a scenario, respecting their wishes should be the priority. Another example of this is the wave of White guilt that followed the 2020 murder of George Floyd in America and the subsequent focus on racial injustice. Many White people, albeit with good intentions, chose this time to reach out to Black people who they had wronged in the past to try and make things right. I received a few messages myself from people I had long lost contact with. While a well-meant action, it also dragged up old wounds for a lot of people. And, at a time when emotions were running high and the global Black community was already under a lot of stress, it is understandable that someone might not appreciate being reminded of a racist microaggression they experienced from a former co-worker many years ago, when they themselves have long since moved on.

That is not to say that it is ever, in the words of One Republic, too late to apologise. It can still be beneficial to take accountability for your actions long after the fact, and this is sometimes needed to bring peace to the affected individual or group. But, for want of a more eloquent phrase, just read the room. Put yourself in the other person's shoes and consider whether the apology will benefit them more than it will yourself. If the answer is no, then this is likely something you should keep to yourself. Or if you're unsure, ask if they have the capacity to consider your apology first. The rule of thumb is that you seek to cause more good than harm.

It's also not helpful, and is actually detrimental, to apologise just to try and alleviate the impact of rejection and bad news. The urge to apologise before letting someone down is a common one – for example, you might apologise before breaking up with someone or having to turn down social plans due to time constraints. We tend to do this because we are genuinely remorseful for the impact that our choice will have on the person. However, the next time you're in such a situation, remember that there is evidence to show that apologies have no impact on hurt feelings (Freedman et al, 2017). In fact, providing such a caveat can lead some people to then not feel comfortable enough to express their true feelings in return, because they feel a pressure to be amenable (Freedman et al, 2017). Unless you have actually done something wrong to the person you are rejecting (maybe some of the failings in the relationship are due to wrongdoing on your part, or you weren't initially honest with your friend about your capacity to hang out), it's usually best to be direct.

Read the room

In general, we just shouldn't apologise when we haven't done anything wrong, even if the apology has positive intentions. This also includes taking accountability for the wrongdoing of others. If you're not involved in what occurred, this is likely to affect the quality of the apology, as it will not be an honest admission of guilt. Doing so also puts you under unnecessary stress and allows someone else to avoid accountability for the harm caused. You may also damage your relationship with the affected party for no reason and do them a disservice in the long run if they were to discover your deception. There are many ways that you can demonstrate empathy and care to those who need it, without giving an insincere apology.

If you do feel that you owe someone an apology, there are a few things to look out for in order to ensure that it comes across as sincere and genuine, so that your apology will have the desired impact.

The first is to ensure that you are specific and explicit about who your actions affected, and how. Failure to include this information implies that the motivations behind the apology may be performative, that it is not truly meant. This does not require a step-by-step breakdown with a twenty-slide presentation and granular detail, just a clear acknowledgement of why the apology is required in the first place, and who it is directed towards.

In a similar vein, it's important to take care not to include dismissive statements that minimise the person's feelings. For example, saying things like 'I didn't expect you to get angry' or 'I'm sorry you felt that way' or getting exasperated if their response isn't what you expected, and saying things like: 'I said I'm sorry, OK.' An apology should serve to validate how the affected person authentically feels about what has happened and provide adequate space for them to express that. Any attempts to suppress that, or minimise the harm caused, are harmful and counterintuitive.

When we give apologies that lack intention or dismiss the other person's feelings, it's usually because we lack a sufficient awareness of the situation at hand. This usually occurs when we rush to apologise in order to try and rectify a situation as quickly as possible or mend a relationship. We can counter this by simply taking a moment to try our best to provide an apology that is considered. Ask yourself if you understand exactly who you have wronged, how you wronged them and how you might have made them feel. What was the extent of the consequences of your actions? Self-questioning in this way will help ensure that you are adequately prepared to deliver an apology sincerely.

A sincere apology should also demonstrate an intention to make things right and ensure that the grievance won't happen again. Apologies that lack this detail can appear hollow and are less likely to be considered seriously. This is a mistake that is often made by celebrities and social media stars that gets themselves in hot water. An apologetic written statement or tearful video is usually released in which they express their sincerest regret and ask their supporters for forgiveness. This is great, but then it stops there – accountability has been taken, but with no follow-up. This leads some to feel that they have been misled and that the individual in question is not genuinely sorry, but only saying they are to save face and protect their platform. The result is a loss of authenticity, and this is a trap that we can all fall into in our haste to express our regret. It sounds obvious, but you can't make things right without actually trying to make things right.

This doesn't necessarily mean correcting the harm caused, though this should be done, if possible. We can also state what we'll be doing to help the person get through whatever situation we may have put them in, or what actions we will be taking to ensure that what we did won't occur in the future. Doing this is a demonstration of sincere care.

Sincere apologies should also not include attempts to justify our actions but take full accountability with no exceptions. This means avoiding phrases such as 'I'm sorry but ...' and 'apologies, however, this is why ...'. It is OK to express that the harm caused wasn't our intention, but it's important to take full responsibility for the impact of our actions. Statements like these indicate a lack of genuine regret and are not empathetic. Sometimes it can be helpful for the person to whom we're apologising to know the driving reasons behind our actions. But we should only provide these if asked.

Apologies can also come across as insincere if they are excessive in nature, and don't match the extent of the grievance. For example, getting overly emotional, or causing a public scene, in response to someone at work letting you know that they felt you had been microaggressive towards them. This is definitely something you should apologise and try to make amends for but being excessive in your response carries the risk of making the situation about you, when your apology should be centring the needs and emotions of the affected person. Doing this can also potentially cause people to feel that they, in turn, have to apologise to you. That is harmful and also does the individual a disservice, if they have made the effort to let you know that you wronged them in some way.

162

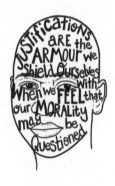

If you have done, or go on to do, any of these things, understand that you are not alone and that this is a reflection of your humanity. It is very normal not to want to be seen as a bad person by others, and having our flaws highlighted can even make us emotional and send us to a dark place. It's incredibly hard and brave to willingly put yourself in a vulnerable place where your character will be questioned. Justifications are the armour that we shield ourselves with when we feel that our morality may be questioned, but it's important to resist this urge. For an apology to be sincere, we need to allow ourselves to be as open and selfless as possible.

> **66** Take responsibility for the impact
> of your actions, regardless of intention **99**

So, with all of that taken into account, here are the three essential steps to form a sincere apology:

1. *Accept wrongdoing, with no caveat provided.* Don't over-think it, a regretful 'I'm sorry', or 'I apologise' are extremely effective.
2. *Take responsibility for the impact of your actions, regardless of intention.* Be explicit about who was harmed and to what extent.
3. *Express how you are going to rectify the situation and/ or ensure that it will not happen again.* Provide tangible examples if possible.

That's it.

Once you have given the sincerest, most complete apology possible, it's then important to let it go. While apologies are effective in mending and nurturing broken relationships, those factors should not be the aim of giving them, but rather a desirable potential outcome. When we give apologies with the expectation of thanks or forgiveness in return, they become an insincere means to an end. We may even be tempted to manipulate the apology to try and engineer a desired response – and that is when we're more likely to behave in a way that is performative, inau-thentic and ultimately unkind. So think of an apology like a present: it's something you give to someone else; it's for them, not you. If you do receive forgiveness, acknowledge and validate the effort that has been made to offer this; express thanks, but remember it is not owed.

If you receive confirmation that the apology has not been accepted, it can be helpful to ask why, as it may have been incomplete, and this is something you could work to rectify. But if this isn't the case and the people concerned simply can't forgive you or move past it, then let it go. Leave the door open for reconciliation in the future, if possible, but otherwise, move on.

Remember to still follow through with your expressed intentions to make things right and ensure that you don't make the same error in future. This is important to do, regardless of the status of the relationship following the apology. Not only is this required for the apology to be sincere, but this is also beneficial for you as a person. Stick to your word and follow through, you'll be all the better for it.

Finally, remember to affirm yourself. The mistakes we make are not a reflection of the quality of our character or our inherent worth. They're just a symptom of being human.

12

Why we should listen to others and be empathetic

Quick question – and be honest. How many times do you ask someone how they are and actually mean it? Of the occasions when you enquire about someone else's wellbeing, how many times do you want the honest answer? I don't ask this question to make you feel bad or to call you out because if your answer is 'few and far between' or 'not as much as I think I should', you're not alone. It's quite common and normalised to have go to phrases that we ask as a form of surface-level small talk, to be nice and pleasant to others.

For example, in the UK it is customary to say 'How's it going?', or 'How are you?' An Irish alternative may be 'what's the craic?' Ghanaians say '*Eti sen?*', which directly translates to 'How is it?' In many corporate work cultures, an email is incomplete without a cheery 'hope this email finds you well?' at the start. Behind these questions lies a genuine intention to demonstrate care and interest for the welfare of whoever we're speaking to. But part of this routine and social dance is also the safe, comfortable answer from the person who has been asked. The provision of an upbeat 'I'm great, thanks', or 'not too bad, ta'.

What this does is allow us to provide an illusion of care without having to necessarily follow through and give it. It keeps things pleasant. This is ultimately unkind, but arguably understandable because our lives can be hectic and fast-paced, with a hundred different things to attend to. We don't always have the time and emotional capacity to take on the weight of someone else's problems. I used to work at a hectic media firm and as much as I enjoyed a good chat by the coffee machine, it had to be at a convenient time, like when I was on a break, looking to avoid doing work, or wanted to miss a boring meeting. If I had deadlines or pressing client pressures, it was a different story. Jane, I'm so sorry that your pet dog has arthritis, but my emails are calling so I'm going to have to give you a polite smile, a half-hearted 'there, there, I'm sure he'll be all right' and keep it pushing.

Getting comfortable with doing this may improve our efficiency, but it comes at a great cost to the relationships that we have with those around us. Because we're not taking the time and making the effort to actually listen, and listening is essential for connection. When we don't provide the space for people to authentically express how they feel, and also feel truly heard, our relationships are likely to be based on unsturdy, superficial assumptions about each other. This is counterintuitive to developing strong bonds; you can't relate to and support what you can't truly see.

For example, Jane is less likely to mention her poorly dog the next time I see her because I dismissed her feelings the first time she tried. If I am looking to become friends with Jane, there's now a substantial side to her life that I will not be privy to, because I don't seem to care. This not only means that I understand her less, but it also means that I can't potentially be there to support her if needed.

So if we want to build stronger, more authentic bonds with those around us, we need to learn how to listen, and practice this often. When we choose to listen to one another, we are giving each other one of the most precious gifts that there are – our attention and time, which are both invaluable. Take a moment to think about the best listener you know and how they make you feel. You may describe this using words like *warm, seen* and *validated*. The simple act of listening, and giving our time to others, can empower them to feel fully realised and believe in their inherent worth. There is so much power to be found in listening, as a skill.

The type of listening that benefits our relationships and allows us to be there for one another is specifically compassionate listening. Compassion means to 'suffer with', so when we demonstrate compassion towards others, we are looking to share in their emotions and help alleviate their suffering by carrying some of the load. In a similar way, compassionate listening is when we listen in a way that enables us to truly understand what someone is experiencing, so we can share the experience with them. Buddhist monk Thich Nhat Hanh also describes this as deep listening, which to him has one purpose: 'to help him or her to empty his heart' (Oprah.com, 2010). Similar to popping a pesky pimple, compassionate listening helps to relieve some of the pressure of the situations that those around us are having.

Compassionate listening requires us to be fully present when others are sharing. This means making an intentional decision to avoid listening to respond. Listening to respond is when you are filtering through what someone is saying as they are speaking. In order to highlight the parts that are relevant to you and work out how you should respond. This is an essential skill for the pace of modern-day life, where there is often minimal time for reflection. For example, if you are working in a busy office or running a hectic family home, listening to respond is the most effective way to navigate several different complex issues at once, and ulti-mately get stuff done. However, when we listen to respond, by definition we are not giving others our full attention and are also centring our needs above theirs. This benefits the pace and effectiveness with which we can solve problems but has a detrimental impact to understanding.

It's similar to when you're reading a book or listening to a song, and your mind wanders, either because you've been reminded of something or have got distracted. It's usually incredibly hard to move on – you're likely to choose to go back a page or restart the track, so you can fully engage with what you're consuming. However, unlike a book or song, when people repeat themselves, it doesn't always have an identical impact, especially if they get a sense that you weren't really listening the first time. It's important to be present.

Similarly, compassionate listening means avoiding the urge to try and problem solve. The temptation to do this often comes from a place of positive intention, and a want to help others. However, when we rush to try and provide solutions without being asked, the impact can be incredibly dismissive. More often than not, when people are choosing to share emotional experiences they're having, they just want someone to talk to who will make them feel heard and help them to feel better about the situation. Not a fix-all solution. Trying to slap a plaster on the problem can make it seem like you're eager to have the interaction be over as soon as possible, which is not compassionate. In addition, if we are coming up with solutions then we are likely listening to respond. So, unless explicitly asked, we should try to leave our toolbox to the side when others are speaking and focus on creating as much space for them to express themselves as possible.

Listening compassionately also means listening to understand, without judgement or criticism. When we place our own perspectives and beliefs onto others, we risk challenging, rather than validating their experiences. Validation is incredibly important. If we don't think that someone truly believes what we're saying and how we're feeling, we're unlikely to feel supported by them. We're also likely to have detrimental feelings of self-doubt and insecurity. So it's key that we disregard our own opinions when listening to others, at least for that moment, and try to see things from their point of view. This doesn't mean that we can't challenge people from a place of kindness, but there is a time and a place for this, and that's usually not when someone is sharing their feelings with us. Furthermore, we cannot adequately challenge if we don't have a sufficient understanding of what we are challenging first, so this should always be the priority. While listening compassionately, any questions that we ask should come from a place of open curiosity. We should be trying our best to seek a deeper understanding of what is being expressed.

We get better at being able to listen compassionately when we increase our capacity for empathy. Empathy describes the ability to share in the emotions of others, so is, therefore, an essential prerequisite to being compassionate. This can be hard to do as when reaching for empathy we can often fall short into sympathy instead. This is when we feel for someone, rather than feeling with them. It's possible to feel bad for someone without truly understanding or relating to what they have going on. This usually sounds like: 'It's sad that happened to you.' Sympathy isn't necessarily harmful, but it presents an obstacle to true understanding and authentic connections.

Professor Brené Brown, in her TED Talk, 'The Power Of Vulnerability' (2010), describes the difference, using the example of someone falling down a hole. Expressing sympathy is akin to peeking into the hole to say: 'Wow, it looks rough down there, sucks to be you!', while empathy is like climbing down into the hole to join the individual and provide comfort. Empathy is just infinitely more effective at building bonds and providing reassurance and support to those who need it. Research indicates that we are most drawn to people who are highly empathetic and tend to trust them more (Morelli et al, 2017). While sympathy keeps people at arm's length, in a manner that just isn't as supportive, so we are less likely to feel closer to those that express it. Even if they are trying to be kind.

Brown argues that we are more likely to offer sympathy when we are afraid of being vulnerable and open with others, about who we are and how we feel. Therefore, increasing our capacity for empathy, compassion and compassionate listening, requires a willingness to be more vulnerable. There is a certain truth to this. If empathising means sharing the emotions of others, then we can't effectively do this without being aware of our own. This requires us to be honest and brave about how we feel and the experiences that we have gone through. We may even have to take ourselves back to dark, sad and trying times in our lives in order to do this. While it is understandable that we cannot always do this for the sake of our wellbeing, it makes sense that a radical level of honesty and openness is beneficial to being empathetic.

True empathy is sometimes an unrealistic ideal that we cannot achieve. If someone expresses to you that one of their parents has unfortunately passed and you are lucky enough to have never experienced a significant bereavement in your close family before, then even a willingness to be vulnerable will not enable you to overcome this lack of shared experience. It will sadly hamper your ability to be truly empathetic. That doesn't mean that we shouldn't always try our best to be compassionate in how we listen and engage with others. But we should also give ourselves some grace, because sometimes sympathy is all we can realistically give.

In the spirit of trying our best to be empathetic and listening to others with a sense of compassion, a practical thing we can do is learn to avoid certain phrases and behaviours that lack empathy. This can enable us to override our less-empathetic instincts and develop new, positive empathetic habits.

The first thing to avoid is trying to find the silver lining when someone tells us about something tough or hard that is happening to them. For many this is an automatic reflex. If someone says, 'The airline lost my luggage and I had nothing to wear on holiday', then a response like, 'Well at least you got to buy a lovely new wardrobe!' would be a silver-lining retort. Just like if someone said, 'My car didn't start this morning', a well-intentioned response might be, 'Well I'm sure the walk did you good'. When we do this, it seems like we're being helpful, when the impact is actually dismissive. We're implying that the individual shouldn't be as upset as they are about what has happened to them. When, even if there is an upside to their scenario, their feelings about it are still valid and important.

Phrases such as 'it could be worse', or deciding to tell the story of something that happened to you that was even more terrible, have a similar impact. The struggles of others don't invalidate our own, there will always be someone else who is experiencing greater hardship. This should moti-vate us to practice gratitude, but we can still be grateful without diminishing our feelings, or the feelings of others. Additionally, telling a personal story in an attempt to relate to the person sharing is also more harmful than we may realise. In an attempt to demonstrate understanding, we can end up just making the situation about us. We can let people know that we relate to what they're going through, without telling a personal anecdote that pulls focus away, unless they specifically ask us to.

It's also advisable not to tell people how they should feel about a situation but allow them to express this themselves authentically. One of the worst things you can do when anyone is emotional is tell them to calm down. I think I can say with confidence that, in the history of the human race, this is something that has rarely worked. This action is very dismissive and indicates to the person that you don't care about what they have to say. If you do feel that someone is getting worked up to a detrimental extent, it's best not to patronise but give them the time and space to settle themselves.

Finally, don't cut conversations short without explana-tion. We can do this when someone starts sharing because we are time-poor and have pressing deadlines. Or because we're feeling uncomfortable, or just don't have the emo-tional capacity to empathise on that particular day. In these situations, it's OK to stick to your boundaries but it's kind to also let the other party know what these are rather than making up an excuse and walking away. Remember that vulnerability and honesty actually help us increase our capacity for empathy and connection with others. Simply expressing the reason why you aren't able to engage with someone on a topic or issue they are facing is a kind way to look after yourself while still showing care.

Compassionate listening is also a skill like any other, so it's something that we can actively practice, and hopefully get better at.

These are some practical tips you can use to improve this skill:

- *Try and learn empathetic phrases that you can simply drop into conversation to indicate to others that you are listening to understand and that they are seen.* Some examples: 'I understand how that would be really tough for you', or 'That's such a difficult situation, I can see how you'd find it hard to deal with.' Or even, 'That sucks – I'm here for you.'

- *Practice asking open-ended questions, rather than presumptuous ones.* For example: 'How are you feeling about it?' 'Can you unpack that a bit more?' and 'What was the impact of that happening?' Rather than: "So you must be angry then?', 'I assume this happened next' or 'I'm guessing this was their reaction.' When listening compassionately, the aim of the questions we ask is to help us to learn more about the person's experiences, rather than confirming our preconceived assumptions. So, practice giving others the space to unpack.

- *It's also useful to practice being comfortable with silence and having lulls in conversations.* This not only ensures that we're not rushing to respond and potentially cutting others off, but it also creates more space for people to elaborate. We often say more than originally intended if we're given the opportunity to. Try to speak less and get used to being fully present, even when no one is talking.

- *If you're having trouble suspending your opinions and perspective in order to validate the experiences of others, it may also be helpful to practice considering your privilege.* Our privilege can block us from seeing and truly believing in the obstacles that others face, simply because we don't face them ourselves. Overcoming this is as straightforward as challenging your beliefs when you are tempted to question what someone is talking about. Instead of jumping straight to 'I don't see it that way', think 'is there a reason why I may not be seeing it in the same way?'.

- *Practice clarifying what people say back to them, as they go.* So, saying things like: 'My understanding of what you're saying is this' or 'Ah, so you did follow the right procedures.' There's no template to this, but you essentially want to simply restate what the other person is saying in your own words. This is an incredibly validating way to demonstrate that you are fully present, listening and following along. It also provides the other person with the opportunity to provide additional clarification if there is anything that you may have misunderstood – therefore helping to deepen your understanding and increase your ability to be truly compassionate.

- *Finally, remember to recognise and affirm the effort that people make when they open up to you.* Ending a conversation by saying 'I'm glad you felt you were able to tell me that', or 'thank you for sharing', lets the person know that you are a safe space for them, and if we all try our best to do this, then our environments will be kinder, more compassionate places to be in.

13

Why we should respect how people want to be addressed

Let's discuss pronouns.

Specifically personal third person pronouns, which, in the English language, are used to refer to people when we don't want to keep saying their name. The two sets of pronouns that are most typically used are he/him and she/her. So instead of saying 'Benjy loves noodles, it's Benjy's favourite meal and something Benjy is always in the mood for', pronouns allow us to say 'Benjy loves noodles, it's his favourite meal and something he is always in the mood for'. (It's true.)

He/him and she/her are pronouns that we typically relate to gender. If someone is a man, we are likely to assume that their pronouns are he/him, and if someone is a woman, she/her. But in reality, it's not that simple.

Gender is a socially constructed phenomenon that varies across societies and throughout history. What it means to be a man or a woman is not fixed, unlike sex, which relates to fixed biological attributes. Because of this, we all develop our personal relationship with our body over time and relate to our gender identity in different ways. As a cis man, how I relate to my manhood is not the same as how other cis men relate to theirs. It's through this individual relationship that some people realise that they are trans and are a different gender to the one they were assigned at birth. Or non-binary, which describes people who don't fit into any gender.

Non-binary people may therefore feel that they're not comfortable being referred to as either he/him or she/her but should be referred to using pronouns that aren't typically related to any gender, such as they/them. Or they may like to be referred to in a less gendered way sometimes, and more of a gendered way other times. If so, they may have pronouns that are a combination, such as he/they or they/she.

There are also some cis people who have a relationship with their gender identity that means that their pronouns are also they/them, a mix, or even ones that are typically related to another gender.

Some people regardless of gender, don't align with he/him, she/her, or they/them at all. Such individuals may use their name as their pronoun, or neopronouns. Neopronouns are gender-inclusive pronouns that have come into prominence in more recent times than he/him, she/her and they/them. For example, *ey/em/eir* are a set of neopronouns that was created in 1975, and the singular gender-neutral '*thon*' was coined in 1858 and included in the *Merriam-Webster* dictionary in 1934 (however it has since been removed). Another example of neopronouns are noun-self pronouns, where a word is used instead, such as cup/cupself. In some online communities, some people also have emoji-pronouns, where a certain emoji is used instead of the pronoun.

So we're therefore not able to assume that because someone has a certain gender identity, or we perceive them to have a certain gender identity, they therefore use certain pronouns. We can't ascertain gender identity from looks, and pronouns also don't necessarily indicate gender identity either. Despite this, it is important that we try our best to use the right pronouns for the people we speak about. Because that is how they would like to be referred to and respecting this shows that we care and value them as human beings. This also means that if people use pronouns that are a combination, such as he/they, we should have a balanced approach to using each pronoun, rather than defaulting to the one that is our personal preference.

This can sometimes be tricky to remember and it takes practice, especially if you have known someone for a long time and they've informed you of a change to their pronouns recently. Or if someone uses neopronouns that you're not familiar with using or pronouncing. But the personal difficulties that we may have don't justify arguing with people about their pronouns or mocking them just because we're not used to them. To do this to someone is to intentionally seek to invalidate their identity and imply that you don't respect their freedom to be authentically themselves.

That may seem slightly dramatic to someone who is

cis and uses the pronouns that are typically aligned with their gender. But that's because this is, in itself, a form of privilege. If your pronouns are the ones that the majority of the world would assume you have, you're likely not to have had many experiences where you've had to correct someone or teach them how to refer to you. Which is often a common occurrence for those who don't have this privilege. Or had someone argue that you're in the wrong or confused about how you should be referred to. Once you take on the perspective of those who do face such obstacles, it becomes clearer how the correct use of pronouns is an act of kindness that has a significant positive impact.

Pronouns are arguably even more important for people who are trans and non-binary. For such individuals, the pronouns they have can also be gender-affirming. They can be a way for such people to anchor themselves in their gender identity and express this to the world. Referring to trans and non-binary folk with the wrong pronouns is often called misgendering, which is a form of microaggression. Misgendering can cause and magnify feelings of gender dysphoria, which describes the feelings of unease and discomfort that some people can have with their gender, in relation to their sex. So, for example, a trans man who uses he/him pronouns may feel gender dysphoria if referred to with she/her pronouns. Something that may on the surface seem like a slight misstep can lead to significant negative consequences. Likewise using the right pronouns for non-binary and trans people can have a significantly positive impact called gender euphoria. This is when you feel connected to and comfortable in your gender, in relation to your sex.

In this way, we can use pronouns as a form of gender affirmation, to help support and uplift the trans and non-binary people in our lives. Research indicates that gender-affirming acts, such as using the right pronouns, significantly improve the wellbeing and mental health of trans women (Glynn et al, 2016). A 2020 US study also found that LGBTQIA+ youth who regularly had their pronouns respected attempted to take their life at half the rate of those who didn't (The Trevor Project, 2020).

Ultimately, making an effort to ensure that we use people's correct pronouns can go a long way in making people feel valued, supported and seen. This has a greater impact on trans and non-binary individuals but is a positive act of kindness that benefits everyone regardless of identity. It's never a good feeling when you are referred to incorrectly, such as being addressed by a different name to your own, so we can all relate to this feeling of wanting to be addressed correctly.

It's important that we are kind to ourselves

However, mistakes do happen. Despite our intentions, there are many reasons why we may fall short of this ambition. Maybe because we are tired, busy, getting used to referring to someone new, or we just simply slip up. In such situations, it's important that we are kind to ourselves.

While doing this can cause significant harm, it is unrealistic to expect to never make a mistake. What matters most is how you address it and correct yourself, and the best way to do so, is to barely address it at all. If you misuse someone's pronouns, the best thing to do is simply apologise, and restate what you said using the correct pronoun. It can be tempting to apologise profusely in such situations because we feel bad and want the person in question, or whoever we're speaking to, to know our true intentions. But over-apologising can inadvertently coerce the other person into apologising to you in order to provide reassurance. This can also cause a scene that potentially places greater focus on the mistake made, and the victim of said mistake. Which can be othering and stress-inducing for the person involved. It is always best to quickly apologise, correct and move on.

There are also things we can do to help ourselves, and others, get pronouns right:

- *If you're struggling with pronunciation, maybe if someone has neopronouns, try respectfully asking the individual for help.* This can also be beneficial if someone has pronouns that are a combination and you're not sure how best to balance how you use each pronoun in a sentence. This may feel slightly uncomfortable for you in the moment but experiencing this brief moment of discomfort is preferable to the negative impact of getting someone's pronouns wrong. As long as you are respectful and sensitive in how you ask, the individual will likely be glad that you made the effort to ask also.

- *Try to get used to using the gender-inclusive pronouns 'they/them' when referring to someone whose pronouns you are unsure of.* Speaking about strangers in a neutral way is a safe bet to minimise the impact of any mis-gendering you may be doing inadvertently. However, this should not be done in replacement of using or asking for someone's pronouns, as this can still have a misgendering impact. Doing this also helps promote greater gender inclusion generally. For example, when we use gender-inclusive pronouns when referring to job titles, changing, 'I need a plumber, he should also have a driving licence', to 'I need a plumber, they should also have a driving licence' is a small but effective way that we can challenge gender assumptions when it comes to job roles.

- *Practice if you think that you need to.* For example, if you've known someone for a while and they inform you of a change in pronouns, this is something that is likely to take you time to get used to. You can quicken the process by simply trying to refer to them more in your day-to-day life or think of them within the context of their new pronouns like thinking: 'I wonder what Robin is up to today, I hope he's happy and does what's best for him.' This is also something you can do to get better at pronouncing pronouns that you're not used to using. There are video and audio tutorials that you can find online on sites such as YouTube that are incredibly helpful if you need to brush up on your pronoun pronunciation skills.

189

- *Speak up if you hear that someone's pronouns have been misused.* Maybe you are at school and hear a fellow classmate use the wrong pronouns for someone you know, or someone refers to someone incorrectly in a work meeting. Often such mistakes are unintentional and informing the individual that they have made a mistake gives them an opportunity to correct it, and means they'll be less likely to do so again in future. It also signals to those around you that pronouns are an important thing to get right. The act of doing this can be incredibly helpful to people who are more likely to have their pronouns misused, as the weight of having to constantly correct people can be burdensome. However, it's also important to keep in mind that doing this can also 'out' people. Just because someone has informed you of their pronouns, it doesn't mean that they have been comfortable enough to tell everyone, so be sure to exercise caution.

- *Try to normalise asking people what their pronouns are when you first meet them.* This ensures that you are referring to them correctly from the start. An easy way to do so is to simply share your pronouns first, e.g.: 'Hi, I'm Benjy and my pronouns are he/him, nice to meet you.' People will usually share their pronouns in response, and if they don't, it means they may not be comfortable to, which is OK also. Doing it in this way also means that you're prompting everyone for their pronouns, not just people who you think aren't cis. If we only ask certain people, this can have an othering, objectifying impact, so it's best to have an equal approach. When more of us share our pronouns, it also normalises the discussion of pronouns, which benefits everyone.

- *You may also want to think of processes you can embed within your environments that encourage the sharing and use of peoples correct pronouns.* For example, I have worked with organisations that get everyone to go around and share their pronouns in turn before a meeting starts. Some also encourage their employees to share their pronouns in their email signatures. Lots of social media sites also provide designated fields on your profile, where you can declare your pronouns, so this is something you could do, and encourage others to do the same. With all of these ideas, it is important to remember and consider that pronouns can be a source of anxiety for people who are still navigating their relationship with their gender identity. So the discussion and sharing of pronouns is something we should encourage, but not force if people are not comfortable.
- *Don't describe pronouns as being 'preferred pronouns'.* Everyone's pronouns are how they prefer to be referred to, however using this language can imply to some that people's pronouns are up for discussion and debate, when they are not. So simply referring to them as pronouns is most appropriate.

The importance of referring to people in the correct way also extends to names. Our names are an important part of our identities; we all know that prospective parents

191

often spend hours poring over name books to pick the perfect one for their child. It's common to be named after a family member, and in many cultures, names have deeply significant meanings. So, when we pronounce or write someone's name incorrectly, this can have a similarly invalidating impact to misusing someone's pronouns. Slipping up once or twice is understandable but having this happen consistently can make people feel othered and lesser-than. As a child, I used to be so thankful when it came time for the school register that I was lucky enough to have a name that was fairly straightforward to announce. Some of my classmates of colour were not so lucky, and you could see the embarrassment caused when another teacher stumbled over their name. Sometimes to such a disastrous extent that it would spark laughter from the other children in class.

This mistake is arguably understandable when it comes to names that are from cultures we're not from or used to. So as a White British person in the UK, you may be forgiven for struggling with saying a name that is common in Nigerian cultures. However, for people who are members of marginalised ethnic groups, the mispronunciation of their name just amplifies the othering that they experience already. It implies that their name is somehow less 'normal' than others. So, while this may be an understandable mistake to make initially, it is something we should try our best to overcome, for all names but especially those of people from marginalised backgrounds. A 2019 UK study found that applicants with distinctly non-British names had to send 60% more applications to be successful than applicants with distinctly British names, despite having the same CV and applying for the same role (The GEMM Project, 2019). This is an example of a bias that we inadvertently contribute towards when we misuse certain names more than we do others.

Giving people nicknames without their permission can also have a similarly invalidating impact, regardless of identity. To ensure everyone feels valued we should be making an effort to address people by the name that they go by and would like us to use, while encouraging others to do the same. There are a few useful ways we can make this easier for us and others:

- *Make a habit of asking new people you meet what their preferred name is.* This can be helpful in environments such as the office, as people can often prefer to be called by a name that isn't on their official documentation. This is also a helpful way to identify whether someone has a nickname that they like to go by.

- *If you recognise that you are likely to have difficulty pronouncing someone's name, try to respectfully ask them if they can show you how to pronounce it.* They will likely appreciate the gesture, and if you've had to ask, then it's likely that you're not the first person to do so. Once you ask, make sure to practice and learn the pronunciation to get it right. Something that can be useful is if you write the name down phonetically (so how it literally sounds). Similar to pronouns, there are also helpful video and audio resources you can find online to help you pronounce difficult names. Looking up interviews is a great hack if you're not sure how to say a celebrity's name, for example.

- *If you want to avoid ever using the wrong name for someone over email, the easiest thing to do is to copy and paste the name that they have signed off their email to you with.* Works a treat every time.

Respecting how people want to be addressed is a small but impactful way that we can be kinder and more inclusive to others. It's tricky sometimes and takes practice but doing this essentially hinges on the principle of trying our best to ask or find out, rather than assume. The time and effort that we put into doing so can go a long way.

14

Why we should uplift
and empower,
not compare and
tear down

No one will say it, so I will – it's not always easy to be happy for others. This feels like an extremely taboo thing to confess out loud, but it's my truth and I don't think I'm alone in this. Some may say that this is a character flaw, but I'd argue that it is just a natural result of the world and times that we're living in currently.

Speaking from my personal experience as a Black person who grew up in predominantly White spaces, I have always felt myself being constantly compared. Not just to the White people around me, to whom I was naturally contrasted, but to other Black people – the few that were in the room with me and also those who weren't. This is the objectifying impact of being part of a group that is underrepresented. You're often not able to just be yourself without having to represent your identity also, and with this often comes a sense of competition.

Say you're the only Black person in a company. In such a situation, you're likely to bear the brunt of any stereotypes and preconceived assumptions that the non-Black people in your company have about Black people. You may also feel like you have to work a bit harder than everyone regardless of your skills and experience, just in case anyone looks to question your position. Now imagine if you are one of only two Black people in a company. You will still have to experience the aforementioned, alongside the feeling that you're now probably, subconsciously or consciously, being viewed in direct comparison with your Black colleague. You're both anomalies of your environment, which draws attention. If your company then has an opening for two managers, and both yourself and your Black colleague go for the role, even if many others are going for it, you may still feel like you're in direct competition with the former, more so than everyone else. As someone who is marginalised and underrepresented, you are one of a few in your environment, and your opportunities may therefore be slimmer than that of other people. Otherwise, why aren't there more of you? Even if you can't pinpoint the reason why there is a lack of adequate representation in your company, it's understandable to reach the conclusion that people like you may not find it easy to thrive there. So if there are two of you going for two open roles, you may fear that they will pick only one of you, or none at all.

The example I've given is rooted in the experience of being from an underrepresented group and feeling tokenised as a result. But the underlying driver of this phenomenon is the competition that usually comes with comparison. This is something that can also be found in the experience of dating. As an eligible single person, if you meet another eligible single person who you like, you're immediately placed in a pool of comparison. That person is likely out and about, potentially meeting new single people every day. They could also be on dating apps at the same time, swiping left and right on hundreds of profiles. Even if you swap numbers with the person and start dating them, until you have the often dreaded 'what are we?' conversation, you may be compared with tens, possibly hundreds of other people. It's daunting but it's true. Thinking about this could cause your mind to slip into competition mode. How can I be the most beautiful, funny, approachable, version of myself? Are they into me? Are they not? What can I do, say or change about myself to make this work?

So with comparison comes competition, and there are many more everyday examples, like when you apply for a university place after leaving school or try to get a mortgage on a house. We live in a society where we're often pitted against each other to get the things that we want. With winners, naturally, come losers – and who wants to be the latter?

What's worse is the fact that the internet and social media have made it so that we can compare ourselves to others to a greater extent than ever before. With a few taps you can have a peephole into the lives of people you know and even those you don't know. You can see where your ex-girlfriend went on holiday with her current boyfriend or the new car that your bully at school purchased. Depending on where we are in life or how we feel about ourselves, this can make us feel better about ourselves, or a lot worse. Either way, it's very easy to naturally fall into making comparisons, and therefore being competitive. This then makes us less likely to be honest on social media, so as not to seem like we're behind, or not living as great a life as those around us. We are inadvertently making the weight of comparison worse, because not only are we comparing and therefore competing with the people we know online, but also the version of ourselves that we've curated.

I hope it now makes more sense why wishing the best and being happy for others isn't always so easy to do. It's tough when doing so might also mean admitting to yourself that you're not where you're meant to be or hoped to be in life. Or that you're lacking in a certain area of your life or aren't deserving of something you want in comparison to someone else. It may be easier to think negatively about the achievements of others, and maybe even wish them ill will, just to feel better about your position. Alternatively, we may choose to take a passive route, and simply ignore people who we fear are doing better than us or withdraw our support. Especially if, like in the example of being underrepresented at work, we think that it might benefit our life outcomes.

The thing is that such a mindset, while definitely understandable, is ultimately misleading and unproductive. Firstly, because we never truly know what other people are going through. Making judgements based on our own perceptions can often lead us to compare ourselves to falsehoods. Especially on social media where it's typical to upload a glossy, filtered highlight reel of your life. Everyone is a lot happier and glowing online, and even if they aren't, it's impossible to have a complete understanding of the day-to-day lives of anyone who isn't us, even if we feel that we might be able to. Making comparisons is a waste of time that can cause us to think negatively, either about ourselves or others, for no reason.

We are also unlikely to achieve contentment in our lives if we are constantly aspiring to compete with other people.

Because that means that we're not prioritising our own desires and wishes. You'll always be distracted and unfocused if you are constantly looking left and right at what others are doing. You should really be focused on whether you like where you're going. In terms of dating, yes, you may be in competition with others for someone you like but it also goes both ways. Are they someone who you see yourself being with? Is there someone more compatible? We potentially lose sight of making sure that the life we live is right for us if we're always so focused on comparing it to others.

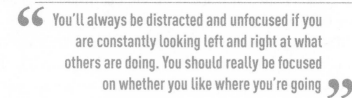

You'll always be distracted and unfocused if you are constantly looking left and right at what others are doing. You should really be focused on whether you like where you're going

Doing this also puts a strain on our relationships and makes us lonely islands of unhappiness. Yes, thinking negatively of the other Black employee in the office may make us feel better about our stunted chances at getting a promotion but at what cost? We have missed out on a potential opportunity for a supportive connection at work while also losing focus on the source of our concern. Our mind should be on the biases present within the organisation that are causing us to feel that our opportunities may be limited compared to others, because of our race. By focusing on comparing ourselves, we have missed out on an opportunity to potentially drive real, impactful change that would benefit us and everyone.

But unfortunately, as mentioned, our society makes it difficult not to compare ourselves to others, and envy is also a very human emotion. To be envious is to feel upset about other people having something that we don't. This is something that we can feel from a very young age, before we know much of anything about the world and how it works. As the eldest child in my family, I remember seething with rage when my younger sibling arrived and I was no longer the sole focus of my parent's attention. To me, this was a great injustice, despite the fact that I was simultaneously elated to have a new playmate at home. But my sibling wasn't going anywhere, so my feelings of envy were something I simply had to put up with and work through. I think this is a process that we can often forget to do as we get older when all we learn is that envy is a negative emotion and an unfavourable trait to have. When we feel envy as an adult, we are more likely to try to push those feelings down or away and try our best not to fully relish in this state of mind.

Instead, I think that taking the time to unpack feelings of envy is ultimately the key to ensuring that we actually process them healthily, and don't end up inadvertently acting on them in a harmful way. When we push how we feel under the carpet, our feelings tend to manifest in other ways. Unpacking exactly why we may be feeling envious and negative towards others can, not only minimise the

203

harm caused in the present, but help us start to change our overall mindset for the future. When we take the time to do this, it usually becomes clear that how we feel is completely about us and has nothing to do with the other person or thing that we're envious of. We're simply projecting our insecurities.

In my case as a child, my feelings of envy weren't the fault of my parents for daring to have another child. Or my sibling for having the audacity to be born. They were just my own infantile feelings of inadequacy, now that there was a newer, cuter baby on the scene. Identifying the root cause of our envy within gives us the opportunity to then self-question and challenge the beliefs that we hold about ourselves. Am I truly inadequate compared to this new baby? Or am I just different? Does the attention that the baby gets genuinely take away from the attention that I get? Is there evidence of this in practice, or is this just an assumption that I've made, based on fear? Am I truly lacking in anything or have I potentially actually gained from this experience?

This process of self-questioning the envy we have towards others in order to redirect our focus away from what we don't have and want, to what we do have and need is also known as moving from a 'scarcity mindset' to an 'abundance mindset'. These are terms that were coined by Stephen R. Covey in his hugely successful book, *The 7 Habits of Highly Effective People* (1989). Scarcity describes having a lack of resources to meet a need and experiencing a scarcity of something can lead us to make decisions and think in ways that we usually wouldn't. For example, the start of the COVID-19 pandemic triggered a massive stockpiling of household goods in the UK and US, with many fearing that the pandemic would cause supply chain issues that would leave them lacking. However, this was a self-fulfilling prophecy. After everyone rushed out to grab what they could, supermarkets were then subsequently lacking in essential supplies because people had bought way more items than they would usually need. This only served to cause further panic, as people who hadn't been as quick off the mark started running out of essentials. This is an example of how scarcity can influence how we think in a detrimental way.

Covey describes people with a scarcity mindset as being so focused on having to win and beat others, that they miss out on the opportunities there are for everyone to win. So to use the example of the toilet paper shortage, the most beneficial course of action for everyone would have been if we all just bought what we needed, and had faith that there would be more when we ran out. But this course of thinking is hard to achieve when we're hyper-focused on getting what we need to survive. We're likely to be less giving to others, to keep our resources to ourselves, and to compare ourselves constantly. We're also typically less mindful, as we have less capacity to think about the here and now because we're so caught up in thinking about what could happen in the future. A scarcity mindset is essentially one that is always panicked and on edge.

A scarcity mindset can come from genuine societal drivers.

For example, people who are low-income are likely to be living in an actual state of scarcity that affects how they think in a way that's ultimately detrimental. A 2013 study found that people who are on low incomes are three times more likely to know the starting point of the taxi prices in their city than those who are of a high income – despite being far less likely to take a taxi themselves (Mullainathan & Shafir, 2013). The feeling that you may not be able to attain something can stop you from considering whether you actually need it. The result is not only a negative toll on your wellbeing due to a focus on the areas where you lack, but the generation of counterproductive thinking that results in the making of counterproductive choices.

In another 2013 study that got participants to order from a restaurant menu (Tomm & Zhao, 2017), half of the group were assigned a high budget and half of the group were assigned a low budget – and the results showed that those with a low budget spent more time looking at the prices than those with a higher budget. So much so, that they were more likely to ignore details such as the food names, calorie content and even miss out on applying the 18% discount on all items that was disclosed at the bottom of the menu. When in a position of scarcity, having a scarcity mindset can lead us to make choices that put us at a further disadvantage.

That is not to say that we can think ourselves out of a lack of privilege – to believe this puts the weight and fault of oppression on the oppressed. However, taking ourselves out of a scarcity mindset can enable us to make choices that are more productive and simply more beneficial for us and others.

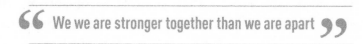

We we are stronger together than we are apart

This means trying to move into an abundance mindset. This is when you are as appreciative as you can be of all that you have and are secure in the knowledge that you are capable of attaining everything in life that is meant for you, regardless of what happens to other people. This allows you to let go of the desire to always compare yourself and compete with others, as their successes don't necessarily take away from yours. Covey describes this as being a win-win perspective. Win-win means that one person's win is to everyone's benefit as it creates more opportunities and generates more resources for everyone to succeed. This is because we are stronger together than we are apart. When we are confident and secure enough to help and empower each other, we are able to create a powerful supportive ecosystem that gets more done. Being in a spirit of abundance means we're more open to sharing and being altruistic and collaborative instead of uptight and competitive. In this way, we're able to work together to achieve mutually beneficial outcomes – this is the core principle of most social justice movements. Bringing this back to the individual, having an abundance mindset also provides us with the calm and mental space we need to focus on achieving what will benefit us and align the most with our desires and values. Rather than coveting what others have, regardless of our needs.

This sounds like an ideal, and in many ways it very much is. Life is hard, and a scarcity mindset is arguably one that can come most natural to us. But there are practical steps we can take, to try to be in a mindset of abundance, as much as possible:

- *Practice gratitude often.* Specifically for the things in your life that you do have in abundance, regardless of your situation. This could be time, familial love, money in the bank, friendships or even access to healthcare when unwell. Making a point to do this often makes us more appreciative of our own lives, and therefore less envious of others.

- *Indulge when you can.* This sounds counterintuitive to overcoming scarcity, however finding small ways that we can treat ourselves, within our limits, is a helpful way to remind ourselves of our worth. Doing this also grounds us in the present, to stop us from hyper-focusing on what may happen tomorrow or what others are doing around us. This could be as small as paying extra for guacamole next time you get a burrito or having a longer lie-in than usual on a Saturday. Find small ways to tap into the parts of your life where you have access to abundance.

- *Try to help people more and give of yourself when you can.* Doing this helps take us away from a place of scarcity into a place of abundance, as, similar to practising gratitude, it reminds us of the excesses in our lives that we may overlook. If we all do this, we can also create structures of cooperation and collaboration that benefit and empower everybody.

- *Be aware of when you are most inclined to compare yourself to others in a negative way and think about what practical changes you can make to limit this.* This could mean spending less time on social media or being intentional about who you choose to follow online.

- *Be as proactive as possible about seeking what you want in life and fulfilling your desires.* Rather than putting energy into wishing that you had someone else's life. As a result of doing this, your life will be full of things that are meant for you, and no one else. But do this with kindness and patience – making small, daily adjustments and investments into the future that you want to have may be more feasible, and that's OK.

- *Don't put an expiry date on your dreams.* Whether you are twenty or sixty, most of us still have many years ahead of us to try and achieve our goals, there is no singular optimum trajectory we need to all be on to be fulfilled and happy. Remember that failure is only temporary, you can usually try again or even try something else. Most of us have the gift of time; this shouldn't be undervalued.

- *Recognise that life pushes us all into a scarcity mindset sometimes and leads us to fall into negative thinking.* That is to be expected because the work of having an abundant, giving and cooperative mindset is a constant one.

Take it a day at a time and be kind to yourself when you fall short.

- *Try saying these positive affirmations regularly.* They will invigorate your life with the spirit of abundance:
- *I share the abundance that I receive.*
- *I deserve to be in a state of constant abundance.*
- *What I want, wants me.*
- *There is more than enough love, blessings and opportunities to go around.*
- *My blessings are limitless.*

15

How we can
be kinder online

Social media is one of the most powerful tools for human connection we have at our disposal. Whether you're looking to keep up to date with your close friends or broadcast a message to the world, there's no method more effective than social media, and there is truly an app for everybody. Platforms such as Instagram, Twitter and TikTok have given us the ability to reach people from around the world and build connections simply by expressing ourselves authentically. They've enabled numerous talented individuals to grow audiences and gain opportunities that they wouldn't have otherwise. Numerous social movements, such as Black Lives Matter and #MeToo have been able to gain greater traction and make a larger impact on our world through the power of social. There are also many cases of injustice which might have gone unseen that have been brought to light because people shared evidence online.

Arguably, social media has brought us closer together and

helped make the world a better place. This is true in many cases, yet the opposite has also happened too; it's made us more distant from each other and had a harmful impact on many. I think this is because our interactions with others online can tend to feel a lot less real and more transient than those that occur offline. You can build connections with people or engage in conflict, without ever having to consider that one day you could meet them. Social media can also provide anonymity if desired. TV shows such as *Catfish* have demonstrated the extent to which you're able to project an entirely different version of yourself out there for others to engage with, if there are things about yourself you'd prefer to keep hidden.

You can also simply choose to have a faceless profile, with no personal details. This is handy for those who are looking to protect their safety, like members of the LGBTQIA+ community who want to engage online with people who also share their experiences but aren't in an environment where they can safely come out, or where they risk being outed. However, for others, faceless profiles are a handy place to hide and dodge accountability for being hateful. Faceless or otherwise, studies show that many users of social media are using it in a way that harms others.

A US survey (Pew Research Center, 2021) found that 41% of adults had experienced online harassment before. Looking into why, 9% of US adults said they had been attacked for their appearance, 8% for their race and 8% for their gender. This indicates that not only is social media a fertile breeding ground for harmful behaviour, but it is also another way for people to express prejudice. Prejudice expressed online can have a significantly detrimental impact on people's confidence, self-worth and wellbeing. In the same study, 25% of US adults said that they'd decided not to share something online for fear of harassment, and 13% had felt forced to leave a platform before, for similar reasons. Additionally, research into hate online against LGBTQIA+ youth in the US found that recipients were likely to have suicidal thoughts, and fear for their physical safety (The Trevor Project, 2020).

It's therefore important that we all, as citizens of the digital world, take on the responsibility of trying to make our online spaces a safer, kinder place for all. This means tackling hate online, and also making sure that we're being kind ourselves. It can be easy for all of us to sometimes forget that behind every username online is a real person, who could be impacted negatively or positively by the words that we type and the actions we take. Forgetting each other's humanity leads us to make harmful or toxic choices, which don't necessarily reflect our character or intentions. To overcome this, we need to be constantly checking in with ourselves, to make sure that we're prioritising the wellbeing of the people we engage with in whatever we do.

However, this doesn't mean that we always have to be positive and suppress how we really feel. Being kind doesn't always mean being pleasant or quiet and there are often situations online where it's important for us to use our voice in a direct way. An example of this might be to hold people accountable for harmful behaviour and challenge those expressing prejudiced beliefs. We can make sure that we're doing the right thing and prioritising inclusion and justice, while also upholding the value of each other's humanity and acting in a sensitive way. It's just tricky sometimes, and we all slip up on occasion.

Here are some practical tips you can use to help you to become the kindest person online that you can be.

Be wary of the information that you engage with and share online

The algorithms of most social media platforms are designed to amplify content that people are engaging with the most. Which makes sense, as this is likely to be content that other people will want to see and be interested in, therefore hopefully creating a more enjoyable experience for all (and keeping people on the app). They'll usually also recommend similar content to users, for the same reason. However, this means that if you engage with content that is harmful, whether it's watching a video, liking, or commenting, this content is more likely to be seen by more people. This means it's crucial that we critically consider what the potential impact could be if someone else saw a piece of content that we're about to engage with, in order to minimise potential harm.

For example, you may see a funny joke on your feed that you'd like to retweet. This is great, the world needs more laughter and joy in it. However, before you hit that share button, it's important to think about whether the joke is harmful or prejudiced in any way. Unfortunately, there is a lot of humour out there that is rooted in prejudiced assumptions and disparaging beliefs about disadvantaged groups, like trans people. These could be seen as innocent humour, however, when prejudice is shared in a humorous way, it serves to normalise such prejudice. This, therefore, makes our online spaces less safe for members of such groups who have to see this content and also makes them more vulnerable offline.

Another example is misinformation, which means information that is partially or completely incorrect and often designed to confuse and misdirect others. Misinformation is rife online and can have a harmful impact on others. There are often stories going around in relation to the quality of certain medical treatments as an example, and how to cure certain ailments. Such stories, if false, could lead people to make health choices that are ultimately detrimental. It's therefore important to verify any information that is claimed to be factual, using multiple authoritative sources, so you're not unintentionally spreading misinformation.

It's also helpful for others online if we report harmful and misinformed content when we see it. Most platforms have content moderation guidelines that users are expected to follow. Reporting such content could not only potentially have them removed from people's feeds, but also result in the source of the content facing repercussions, therefore making all of our feeds safer.

Take a second to think before you act

Things can move incredibly fast on social media. Conversations progress in a matter of milliseconds, trends can blow up then burn out in hours and we're oversaturated with hundreds of news stories a day. We're therefore all incentivised to act quickly and feel we need to respond before a conversation moves on without us, take part in a trend before it's old news, and engage with current events before they are, well, not current anymore. However, moving at speed means that we're taking less time to think our choices through and we're more likely to do something that is out of character and potentially unkind. So, before you do anything, it's worth just taking a moment to think objectively about what the impact of that action could be. How could that tweet you're about to post be received? Is the trend you're partaking in one that aligns with your values? Would you be comfortable saying the same thing offline, to someone's face? Trends come and go but the harmful impact our actions have online could be significantly more permanent, so taking time to think before acting can be a helpful kindness hack.

Disagree responsibly

As much as it would make all of our lives a lot easier, it is unrealistic to expect everyone to agree with our opinions on every topic in the world. With human communication naturally comes disagreement and sometimes conflict, and we need to anticipate this when communicating with people on social media. It's important for us all to stand by our beliefs and challenge harmful opinions, especially hate speech. However, this doesn't justify unkind behaviour, such as the use of abusive language and public shaming, especially as the root cause of many disagreements is simply ignorance. Acting in an uncompassionate manner towards others is not a productive way to come to a common understanding and resolution that benefits everyone. That doesn't mean that we should agree to disagree on every issue – our opinion on topics regarding human rights will justifiably be more absolute than, say, our preferred flavour of ice cream. But we should always ensure that we're engaging in discourse with a sense of care that keeps our online spaces safe for all. This sometimes also means knowing when to let things go. If you can tell that someone is being willfully ignorant and is not discussing an issue with you in good faith, but rather has other malicious intentions, then the best option is often to simply disengage. Pick your battles wisely, soldier.

Use trigger warnings

A trigger warning is something that you use to warn others that they may be about to experience something traumatic that could negatively impact their wellbeing. In the context of social media, this may look like simply saying 'Trigger warning' (or TW), and listing the trigger at the start of a particular post before you share it. Unfortunately, you'll never be able to be completely sensitive to everyone's needs, what may trigger you may not trigger me, and it could be something I hadn't even considered before. But it is just kind to get into the habit of placing a trigger warning before extremely disturbing content or anything that could stimulate a strong emotional response from others. A case in point, it's helpful to share a trigger warning before sharing examples of police brutality. These are often important to amplify but can also be disturbing to watch. Especially for members of demographic groups that are disproportionately impacted by police brutality and other related injustices.

Be wary of pile-ons

It can be fun to engage in social commentary – sharing your opinions and engaging in conversations is a huge part of what makes being on social media platforms enjoyable. But it's important that we always do so within reason, with a consideration of context. Imagine if you came across a video on your feed of an aspiring comedian telling an unintentionally awful joke. Like, really bad, and not in a tongue-in-cheek way. You may feel the urge to put your thoughts underneath the video to express how bad you think the joke was. You could even repost the video to share your thoughts on the quality of the joke and see if your network feels the same. This is arguably understandable. If someone has posted a joke online, it's to entertain others and so they're expecting a certain degree of feedback, positive or negative. As long as you don't disparage the individual's character or appearance, aren't unnecessarily cruel and focus your feedback on the joke itself, it's fair game.

Now imagine the exact same scenario but when you go to comment, you notice that the video already had thousands of comments and it's been shared thousands of times also. The response is also almost all negative, with hateful and unnecessary sentiments being expressed by a number of people. In such a situation, there's probably no need for you to share your feedback as the person likely already knows that their joke was terrible. Not only that, but the weight of disapproval that they're facing already is probably not doing wonders for their self-esteem. The kindest thing to do is to share a message of encouragement, or not add one at all. Remember that there is usually only one person behind each account you see online, and there is only so much negativity one can take without experiencing distress. There are also passive ways to provide feedback on the content you see online, for example, you can report posts that you feel may be harmful.

This applies to everyone, including celebrities and people with huge followings online. It's tempting to think that such individuals are used to experiencing feedback and potential backlash, but this isn't an excuse to be unkind. They may not see your hate message among the many they might receive but on the off chance that they do, it could still affect them negatively. So be considerate and remember also that even if the public figure doesn't see the message, someone in your network likely will. If you are making fun of a celebrity for their appearance, this could in turn also make someone you know feel self-conscious about their own appearance. It's important to be considerate.

Know when to apologise

If, despite your best intentions, you have acted in a way that has negatively impacted someone online, it's important to take accountability for this and apologise. Getting into the habit of doing this not only stimulates environments of mutual care and understanding but also helps us to grow as individuals and refine our digital kindness abilities.

Spread and amplify positivity

Research shows that we can stimulate positive, kind behaviours online through the content that we share. A 2014 study artificially manipulated the emotional content shown in the Facebook feeds of a sample group. Some were served less positive content than usual, and some were served less negative content than usual, and their activity in response was monitored. The results indicated that people who saw fewer positive posts created fewer positive posts, and those that received fewer negative posts produced fewer negative posts (Kramer et al, 2014). This demonstrates that emotional states can be influenced through social media content, so it's good to make the effort to try and share positive, uplifting content when you can. Engage with posts that make you smile and show love to people you know and also don't know. We all have the power to make a positive difference and inspire kindness.

Being the kindest we can be online also means practising self-kindness. We need to fill our cup so we have enough kindness and compassion to give to others. It's also just as important that we take steps to protect our safety and wellbeing online, as we would offline.

Below are some practical steps that you can take to ensure that you're also being as kind to yourself as you can be.

- *Remember that most social media algorithms are designed to amplify content that people engage with to its users and serve them more of the same, and that user group includes you.* This means if you engage with content that triggers you or negatively impacts your wellbeing, you're unfortunately likely to be served similar content in the future. So as a safeguarding measure, try not to engage with content that may disturb you and make liberal use of the report function.

- *Remember that social media is used as a highlight reel for most and is usually not a direct reflection of the lives that others are living.* Try not to compare yourself to what you see online.
- *When sharing your own content, do not consider how it may be received beyond ensuring that you're not causing harm or being insensitive.* Chasing approval and likes online is the quickest route to inauthenticity, frustration and unhappiness. The approval you should value and seek first and foremost is your own. If you take a selfie and you like it, post it! Do it for yourself, you deserve it.
- *Try to monitor your social media use on a weekly/monthly basis.* Spending a lot of time online is not inherently harmful but it can cause your wellbeing to deteriorate if it begins to stop you from making connections with people offline or making the most of your offline life in general. There's nothing wrong with taking a break every now and then, everything in moderation.
- *Be careful about the information that you share publicly.* It's important to be wary about posting details about your life that could put you in danger, such as financial information, or exact details about where you live. It's easier than you think to do this unintentionally, by sharing house tours or taking photos outside your house with the number in view. Always be wary, so you're not unnecessarily exposed.
- *If you have people in your life, online or offline, that you can trust, lean on them if you're ever experiencing harassment or abuse.* No one deserves to suffer alone, and people

are usually as supportive as they have the capacity to be if you ask. Especially if the culprit is someone you work or go to school with. Reporting such behaviour to the respective authorities is the kindest thing you can do, for yourself and others.

- *Utilise your privacy settings.* You don't need to be exposed to the thoughts and opinions of everyone on the internet if you don't want to be. Most platforms have features that allow you to disable comments, and even make your account completely private and inaccessible to anyone who isn't approved. These options are designed to improve your comfort, so make the most of them.

- *Finally, never be afraid to block someone.* There is no reason too small; your social media account is your house and you have the right to accept and eject as you please. There is no shame in protecting your peace. The block button is your friend.

16

Why we should be kinder to the planet

In order to be kinder to one another, we need to consider how kind we are to the world that we all live in. This spinning rock is one of the fundamental things that we all have in common. It's our home and sustains us in so many ways. It's therefore only right that we try our best to repay the favour and sustain it in turn, so we can all continue to enjoy it, equally. Unfortunately, it doesn't look like we're doing a great job of doing that thus far. The Earth is warming up to dangerous levels and it's essential that we reduce the harmful emissions that we emit into the Earth's atmosphere to stop it from getting any warmer.

The issue of climate change can often feel like it's a problem we can afford to delay getting around to solving. It's hard to picture the Earth being completely uninhabitable one day. Trying to envision what that might look like without thinking of overly dramatic Hollywood doomsday blockbusters is pretty tough because it's too removed from many of our realities. This can easily lull us into a false sense of security, that yes climate change is an issue, but probably one that can wait. It's something future generations will have higher on their list of priorities than those of us who are here today. But while it is true that the people who come after us will bear the brunt of the choices we make, climate change is negatively impacting people around the globe right now.

There are so many places in the world that are becoming too hot and dry, or cold and wet, for certain crops to survive, and animals to thrive. This is having a significant impact on people's quality of life and is a source of conflict too. There are also increasing instances of extreme weather such as wildfires, floods, and heatwaves. The result is loss of life, and loss of life quality – 7 million people currently die every year due to illnesses caused by air pollution (UNEP, 2022), and 20 million people become climate change refugees every year too (UNHCR, 2021). A climate change refugee is someone who has been forced to cross an international border as a direct or indirect result of climate change.

This isn't an issue that many people can afford to tackle at a later date, but one that is very much pressing today. Not having to worry about climate change affecting your life in a significant way is a luxury that only the most privileged in the world have. Despite the fact that 86% of CO_2 emissions are generated by the richest half of the world's countries, there is a general trend that countries with less economic power are more likely to be geographically positioned to be most affected by climate change effects (Our World in Data, 2018). For example, the Philippines produce only

0.35% of the world's CO_2 emissions, yet are extremely vulnerable to extreme floods and typhoons, and the rate at which these occur is exacerbated by climate change (Our World in Data, 2018). Countries with less economic power are also less able to adapt themselves to be able to withstand these changes in environmental conditions or rebuild following extreme weather events. In general, our ability to cope with changing climate conditions and climate disasters reflects our income level as individuals. Those with more money have a greater ability to relocate if they need to, for example.

Climate change also has a greater impact on marginalised racial and ethnic groups. In the US, Black people are 40% more likely to live in areas experiencing the highest increases in temperature-related death (EPA, 2021). The Latinx community in the US is also disproportionately vulnerable to extreme temperature increases, due to their disproportionate involvement in weather-exposed jobs. In the UK, People of Colour are also more likely to live in cities where pollution levels are higher, and there is generally less access to green spaces, resulting in increased exposure to related health issues. In 2021, Ella Adoo-Kissi-Debrah was the first person in the UK to have air pollution stated as their official cause of death on their death certificate. She was a nine-year-old Black girl from Lewisham in South East London, not far from my hometown of Croydon.

Hopefully, you can see that protecting the environment is about more than just saving it for future generations, although I'm sure they'll be thankful too. It's an essential requirement if we want to protect the most vulnerable among us today. Luckily, there are things that we can all do to be kinder to each other – by being kinder to the Earth.

The first is to limit the amount of plastic waste that we produce, as almost all plastic is made in a way that harms the planet. UK households throw away an estimated 1.85 billion pieces of plastic waste a week (Greenpeace & Everyday Plastic, 2022), so working on getting that figure down as individuals is one way that we can lessen our impact on the environment. Think about all of the times in your everyday life that you use plastic and consider whether you could use a reusable alternative instead. For example, try asking your favourite takeaway spot to not include plastic cutlery, so you can use the utensils you have at home. If you often forget to bring a tote bag to the supermarket, start putting a reminder on your weekly grocery list. Try to carry a reusable water bottle around with you, they always come in handy, and take a reusable coffee cup to the coffee shop with you. Before throwing away plastic containers, think about ways you can keep and use them again, and try to avoid using plastic straws if you can. However, if you do have to use and throw plastic away, remember to recycle. Sorting through our waste admittedly isn't the most enjoyable of tasks but plastic takes an extortionate amount of time to decompose at a landfill, and landfills are a key producer of harmful warming gases. Therefore, the more plastic we recycle, the better.

It's also helpful to get into the habit of recycling anything that you can. For example, electric waste is the fastest-growing form of domestic waste in the world. Some 53.6 million metric tonnes are produced each year, and this is predicted to reach 74 million metric tonnes by 2030 (Forti et al, 2020). This is unsurprising when you consider our increasing reliance on technology as a society, and how fast technology is developing too. There's always something new and shiny that does a more useful, interesting, or entertaining thing. But before you get your new laptop, games console, or phone, don't forget to recycle your old one instead of throwing it away. Many companies will even reward you for the pleasure, with discounts on your new purchase.

Another way that we can be kinder to the planet is by flying and driving less, as cars and planes are key producers of harmful emissions. Try to walk or ride a bike to get to places if you can, and for your next holiday, think about environmentally friendly travel options like trains. Also, think about having less meat and dairy in your diet. Unfortunately, meat and dairy production is particularly bad for the environment. A lot of water is used, harmful gas emissions are produced and the process can also result in the destruction of natural habitats. As supply is influenced by demand, we can help reduce the need by choosing to consume less. This doesn't necessarily mean going vegetarian or vegan – I must admit that I'm particularly partial to chicken wings, and don't get me started on steak. But we don't necessarily have to have meat with every meal, and there are also many awesome meat substitutes on the market now, especially for products such as mince and sausages. To get started, try having a meat-free Monday or go vegetarian for a month, for practice. It's a lot easier than you think and makes the times when you do have meat, even more pleasurable.

The following tip is one that pains me to write, but it has to be done. We need to buy less fast fashion if we want to fight the climate crisis and protect the environment. It's amazing that we now have the ability to make Friday night party plans on a Thursday afternoon and have a completely new outfit arrive in time to match. The rise of social media and fashion influencers means that trends feel like they come and go so much quicker, and everyone likes to feel good about what they wear. But the speed at which clothing is having to be produced to meet this demand is simply unsustainable. Not only does production emit harmful fumes, but the more we buy, the more we throw away and contribute to landfill. So, whenever you're tempted to hit up your favourite online retailer, try to be kinder to the planet by shopping in your wardrobe instead. It can also help to unsubscribe from any email chains you're on, so you're not sucked in by the promise of another sale. If you do buy something new, try to purchase staples that will last you a long time and go out of style less quickly. Choosing to buy pre-loved at charity stores, and donating your old clothes are also wins for the environment.

Finally, try to be more aware of how much energy you use in your home. For example, turning off lights when you don't need them, and not using the dryer or dishwasher if you don't need to. This is also a great way to save money.

For more helpful tips and inspiration, try to follow people online who talk about protecting the planet and living sustainably. You'd be surprised how much useful content you'll then learn just by scrolling through your feed and doing this helps keep the issue top of mind also. Share whatever information you get with others, too; we all benefit if more of us are eco-conscious. We need to do this while remembering not to judge either, as everyone is on their own journey and it's not a competition. The ability to make choices that are better for the environment can also be a sign of privilege, so this is something that's important to be considerate of.

To give you an example of what I mean by this, think about the fact that many people across the world don't have access to a reliable supply of electricity. Meaning that, in some regions, having a diesel generator is necessary. Such generators are high-emission drivers and not great for the environment, but such individuals are not in a position to make a different choice. You are also typically more likely to have access to a high-quality public transport network if you live in a city. However, the cost of living is also typically higher in cities. Meaning that if you are low-income, you may need to live in an area that is more rural, where you have to drive. Fast fashion is bad for the environment, but it's also very affordable and therefore popular for reasons that aren't just superficial. If you have a low income and urgently need new clothes for work, a fast fashion retailer may be your best bet. It's also easier for people with larger bodies to find brands online that make clothes in larger sizes. Shopping online is also just a more accessible experience in general than shopping in person, and is, therefore, an essential service for people with mobility issues. Mobility issues also mean that not everybody can simply bike or walk somewhere instead of taking the car. Certain reusable alternatives to plastic can also be inaccessible for disabled people. For example, not everybody can drink safely without a straw, and reusable straws often can't be sufficiently sterilised. Metal straws can present a risk of injury and paper straws a risk of choking.

There are many ways that a lack of privilege can mean that someone simply can't make the most environmentally friendly choice in a situation, and it's unkind to ignore this. We thus shouldn't make others feel bad for making choices that we would personally avoid or force people to explain themselves and defend their actions. A lack of privilege is not always visible: you never know what circumstances others may be in. We can have a greater, kinder impact by simply modelling the behaviour we want to see and spreading awareness in a caring way, whenever possible. Especially as making better choices as individuals will not be enough to stop climate change – even though we're often told that it will be.

Conversations about protecting the environment are often centred around monitoring your carbon footprint, that is the amount of greenhouse gas emissions that you produce through the choices that you make. It's difficult to specifically calculate, but the idea is that, if you work towards reducing it by making better choices, you're likely to have less of a negative impact on the environment. Therefore, if we all monitor and reduce our carbon footprints, we should solve the climate crisis. This idea has been around for decades but was popularised in 2005 through an advertising campaign by British Petroleum (BP), which is a fossil fuel company. The campaign was hugely successful and has had a positive impact by providing a helpful way for many to think about being kinder to the environment. However, the burning of fossil fuels is incredibly bad for the environment: 71% of greenhouse gas emissions between 1988 and 2015 were driven by just 100 fossil fuel companies globally (CDP UK, 2017).

So, it's arguably ironic for such a campaign to be pushed by a leader in the burning of fossil fuels, and BP hasn't slowed down since the campaign either. One could say that the campaign may have been a strategic move on the part of BP, rather than an ethical choice to help protect the environment. They may have done so because when we place the sole focus on solving the climate crisis on us as individuals, we're distracted from holding governments and corporations accountable for the part that they play. BP, as a major contributor to the production of harmful emissions, could have a massive positive impact on the environment if it invested in low-carbon and renewable energy sources. At least more than I can have as an individual by deciding to not fly abroad for my summer holiday this year. That doesn't mean that we shouldn't all do our bit to be kinder to the environment, but protecting the environment also means applying pressure where it counts.

It is undeniable that households in the UK produce a huge amount of plastic waste. However, the recycling systems in the UK are also not sufficient to handle the amount of plastic that is recycled, therefore exacerbating the plastic waste crisis. Of the plastic waste that is put into recycling, only about 12% is actually processed, the majority incinerated and buried at landfill sites (Greenpeace & Everyday Plastic, 2020). And while we can have a positive impact by using less plastic and recycling where possible, we could have an even greater one if the UK government worked to improve the recycling systems.

Also, food packaging makes up a significant portion of the plastic waste that's produced, however, consumers don't have control over the packaging their food comes in. Supermarkets could have a huge impact by investing in packaging alternatives that are more easily recycled. There is so much more that can be done by those who hold power and it's clear that governments can help protect natural habitats and plant trees to absorb carbon, if they devote the time and resources to doing so. They can also help insulate more homes, so we don't have to use as much energy to heat them. Collective action is a vital piece of the puzzle that we can't miss.

Use your voice and give feedback to the businesses that you buy things from, asking them to limit their use of single-use plastic packaging. Demand that they consider their impact on the environment, set positive environmental goals and stick to them. Use your voting power to support political representatives who have strong views on climate change. Advocate for environmentally friendly policies and support positive environmental causes. Donate your money or your time if you can.

We all need to stay informed, demand changes and hold those with power to account. We should all be doing our part as global warming is everyone's issue. Therefore, everyone should be doing what they can to be part of the solution.

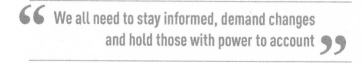

66 We all need to stay informed, demand changes and hold those with power to account 99

17

Why positive change happens in small moments

For me, the gym is a hopeful reminder that small wins can indeed lead to larger victories. When you join a new gym, you're likely to be offered an induction, usually by a keen personal trainer who is hoping to sign you as a new client. If you choose to accept, the orientation will probably feature a tour of the premises, information on what classes are on offer and maybe advice on how to meet your goals and stretch properly. No one comes out of their gym induction looking or feeling like they've been exercising there for a year if they haven't been exercising elsewhere previously. We're not disappointed by the fact that this doesn't happen either. To start to feel the benefits of the gym, you need to go a few times first; this is common knowledge.

Over time, depending on what your goals are, you'll hopefully start to gain small achievements like a personal best on a machine, or managing to consistently attend for a certain amount of time. Maybe you'll start feeling a difference in your muscles and joints or you'll hit some mental health milestones. Whatever your goals are, if you keep going, you should keep achieving, more and more each time. It doesn't stop either. Even if you reach a point where you're happy with the progress you've made, you're likely to make new goals to achieve or put together a plan to help you maintain instead. It's true that you may also face some setbacks or plateaus on your journey. But you keep going regardless. Not even The Rock has worked out enough never to need to exercise again. With further commitment should come further achievement, at least that is what we hope and try to stay committed for.

Thinking about being kind in the same way as going to the gym can make our efforts seem considerably more worthwhile and motivate us to push forward. Yet it can feel like an uphill battle sometimes. When we look around at the state of the world and the suffering and injustices that persist, being kind can seem like a pointless task. The news cycle tells us that as a society we are, for the most part, a prejudiced, cut-throat group of people. Glued to our phones, obsessed with material things and only concerned with pursuing our own interests. It can feel like there are an overwhelming number of social issues to tackle, whether they be systemic oppression, hate crimes, the climate crisis, the cycle of poverty – the list goes on. With not enough people who seem to care about them to make an immediate difference, why should we even try? Before making any decision that may require us to expend our resources, it's practical to complete a cost-benefit analysis. Even with the most positive of intentions, doing such an analysis on being kind can cause us to give up and not try at all. This is because the issues we are looking to tackle seem so huge, bigger than the resources at our disposal.

Even if we are willing to swim upstream, we can often find ourselves frozen in indecision, because there is just so much to consider that we feel overwhelmed. The world feels smaller than ever now, and we have access to the experiences and struggles of more people than any other generation in history. This can be a positive thing yet it can also trigger worry and panic within us. The more we know, the more challenges we're aware of and the more aware we are of the extent to which our actions can impact others. There is a certain safety and comfort that comes with ignorance. You have less on your plate and are less likely to be worried that you may inadvertently cause more harm than good by saying or doing the wrong thing. Being more open to doing good can actually make you more likely to do nothing at all.

A key obstacle to everyday kindness is also simply the struggles of individual life. Many of us are too busy trying to keep our heads above water to look beyond our day-to-day experiences and help others in a way that we think will be meaningful. We don't all have the capacity to go out of our way, all of the time.

But the thing is that, while all of these obstacles are real, we're never facing them by ourselves. There is always someone else besides us who is also trying their best to be kind, do the right thing and have a positive impact on the world. We're never as alone as we may feel in these efforts. Because when we make the time and effort to look for it, our communities are full of altruistic people.

To be altruistic is to care for others in a selfless way. Altruism is the opposite of being selfish and self-concerned. It's when we make the decision to put the needs of others before ours, and most of us are altruistic in some way. For example, we are altruistic in how we treat the people that we love. It's normal to want to have the energy we put into our relationships, platonic or otherwise, be reciprocated in some way. But this is often not what motivates our actions. Many of the things that we do for the people we love, we do because we just want them to be happy and live a good life. This is an altruistic motivation that most of us share.

Most of us are also altruistic in the jobs that we do, meaning that we're not completely motivated by the promise of being paid a certain wage. Money is definitely an important motivator, especially for those with less priv-ilege, but for most, there are usually others. For example, if you're a school teacher, you're likely also motivated by an altruistic desire to inform and inspire the next generation. If you're a professional dancer, you're likely also motivated by an altruistic desire to entertain and delight others. A cab driver will likely gain a sense of satisfaction when they help someone get home late at night. Even those who work out of complete necessity may also be motivated to use the money for altruistic purposes. Maybe to support their family for example.

The COVID-19 pandemic was also a great time for

demonstrations of kindness – not everybody was hoarding toilet paper. Young people checked in on their elderly neighbours and there were virtual games and social media challenges galore to help entertain people struggling with loneliness and isolation. Organisations and individuals alike came out in support of front-line workers. Many of us heeded warnings to stay home to help control the spread, we socially distanced and wore masks when we were outside and got vaccinated in droves as soon as we could. Data indicates that in Britain, during 2020, 0.7 billion more pounds were donated year on year to charities (CAF, 2021). So many people took the opportunity to step up and give what they could to those who needed help during this difficult time in the world's history.

In fact, when we look back in time, there are numerous examples of individuals stepping up to perform brave altruistic acts and uphold the humanity of others. Like Saint Maximilian Kolbe, a Polish Catholic priest who was killed in Auschwitz concentration camp, in 1941. Kolbe was canonised as a martyr for volunteering to give up his life in the place of a stranger, so they could hopefully survive and return to their family. Kolbe's story is one of inspiring strength, benevolence and empathy in the face of adversity. But while it is an amazing one, there are people like Kolbe who we can find at all points of human history, even today.

More people than we think have a genuine desire to support those who are struggling and help make the world a better place. Some contributions may be smaller than others, or simply different. But like achievements in the gym, every small milestone should unlock another, we just have to keep going and keep trying, even if there is no endpoint in sight.

If you find yourself frozen in indecision, or don't know where to start, think first about what you have influence and control over. We all have roles that we play in the world, whether it's our job role, our position in our family, our friendship groups, or in our community. Thus we also have a choice in how we play those roles, and choosing to play them in an as empathetic, caring and kind way as possible can make a huge difference. The size of your contribution doesn't reflect its value or even its potential impact. Such inspirational pillars of altruistic kindness like Saint Maximilian Kolbe did not necessarily know the extent to which their actions would go on to impact others. But not every kind and altruistic act has to involve making such a great sacrifice.

Pick up litter as you walk your dog in the morning, and smile at someone on the train who looks dejected. Get involved in positive community projects and take every opportunity you can to affect change by using your vote. Speak up when you see prejudice occur, join protests and support those who are disadvantaged with every privilege that you have at your disposal. Pour into yourself so you can pour into others and remember to practice self-care by choosing yourself first and having clear boundaries. Just commit to doing good things often, and the rest should flow.

There are also measured ways that we can inform our altruism and approach to kindness that are helpful in driving action. One method is the philosophical belief system called 'effective altruism', posited by thinkers such as William MacAskill. Effective altruism essentially argues that we should base our good works on objective metrics, to ensure we have the most impact with the resources we have on the problems that we are most able to help solve. Websites such as GiveWell are informed by such thinking; they help people find out which charities do the most good with the least money.

It is arguably difficult to measure the value of good, and many positive social good causes that have inherent value, don't result in tangible results that we can see immediately. For example, dismantling oppressive systems is not an overnight task, but is one that, if achieved, will benefit swathes of people. We are also human beings and not robots, so making an objective choice is often unrealistic. The causes we are drawn to will inevitably be informed by our experiences, emotions, relationship ties and how we perceive the world.

66 What is the most impactful way that I can do good in the world, with what I have? 99

But effective altruism does simplify the challenge of being kind and doing good to a simple helpful question: 'What is the most impactful way that I can do good in the world, with what I have?' This takes the pressure off immensely – we all just need to focus on maximising our personal positive output, whatever that is. This includes partaking in both individual and collective action, if possible.

Living by this question also puts the power back in our hands to consider what is right and take a chance on our own judgement. There are objective moral truths, such as it being harmful to kill or steal from others. There are also general principles we can follow in order to be kinder to ourselves and one another, which have been covered in this book. But there isn't one singular way to show care in every situation. Every context is different, and we are imperfect people who live in an imperfect world. We therefore can't live in fear of making mistakes and causing harm in our pursuit of doing good, because that is inevitable. We ultimately need to try our best always and trust our human instinct to know what is right. And we need to be open to learning, changing and putting in the effort to do better. Because it's worth it.

It's worth it for ourselves. Altruistic acts are selfless deeds, but research does show that being altruistic is also beneficial to our mental health (Stern, 2019). When we try our best to support others, our relationship with those around us improves in a way that also benefits our wellbeing. In health, altruistic desires are also a positive sign that you are mentally healthy. (Stern, 2019).

Giving to others also helps us feel more connected and less lonely. When we give, we're reminded that we are needed and that our existence serves a greater purpose. It's a similar feeling to having a pet, a younger sibling or being someone's mentor. Being depended on can feel good and push us to be better people. It also encourages us to look after ourselves, so we are able to give more.

> ❝ We need to be open to learning, changing and putting in the effort to do better. Because it's worth it ❞

It's worth it for those around us too, because kindness is contagious. We are often inspired to be kind by seeing other people be kind, and people who experience kindness often then pass the kindness on. Choosing to be kind, in even the smallest way, can start a chain reaction that goes on to change a system and benefit more lives than you realise. We can all be kindness influencers.

It's also worth it to ensure the survival of the human race and the world. Humans are interdependent beings, as individuals; we aren't able to survive all of the unplanned catastrophes that life throws our way. We need each other. A community that is altruistic, with strong support systems that are rooted in kindness, is a stronger community. Because it's a community where resources are distributed based on need. This means that those who are most disadvantaged are catered for, and everyone is sufficiently supported, so they may then go on to support themselves and others. With kindness and altruism comes justice, justice for our fellow humans and also justice for the planet, on which we also depend.

So lean into every impulse that you have in life to be kind to yourself and others. Do so with bravery, confidence, and compassion. Because through acts of kindness, together we can become a positive force for good.

One that slowly but surely changes the world.

66 Through acts of kindness, together we
can become a positive force for good 99

ACKNOWLEDGEMENTS

I would first like to thank the people who were integral to the publication of this book.

Katie Packer and Feyi Oyesanya, thank you for believing in me as a first-time writer and being such strong advocates for this book. Your guidance and reassurance have been invaluable. Thanks also to Headline and Hachette for your support as a publisher, and Kelsey Robb and Natalie Lyddon from TikTok, who I sincerely appreciate for helping open the doors to this opportunity.

Next, I would like to thank those who inspired the creation and content of this book.

Thank you to my amazing TikTok family who has hung out with me on countless live streams. Our sprawling conversations about the many ways that we can better ourselves and make the world a kinder place are what have inspired many of the themes in the book. You all make the sometimes scary world of social media feel a bit safer and give me so much hope for a brighter future. Thank you to those who appreciate my online content enough to watch, like, share and leave comments. Your support is what has kept me driven. Thank you to all the members of The Collective, the intersectional employee resource group I was a part of all those years ago that helped me find my voice. Thanks also to everyone at Hustle Crew, the incredible DEI consultancy I work for. You have been integral to the development of my career, given me opportunities to grow and have been so supportive of my work.

Finally, I would like to thank everyone who has gotten me to this point in my life.

Thank you to all of my dear friends who I am blessed enough to call my chosen family. You have never made me feel like my voice is too loud or my dreams are too big. I appreciate you all more than you will ever know. Thank you to my sister, Abena, for being a source of advice and inspiration.

Thank you to anyone who has ever said an encouraging word to me or someone they know about who I am and the work that I do. Finally thank you to seventeen-year-old Benjy. Thank you for not giving up on yourself and your life. The decision you made to push against your fear and go through the pain required to become your most authentic self wasn't easy. But look now! It's paying off.

GLOSSARY

Bias

A bias is a preference for or against someone or something. We often develop biases from our personal experiences, the things we're taught, what we see, and the content we consume. Biases can influence the opinions we hold and the decisions that we make.

Cis/Cisgender

Someone whose gender identity aligns with the gender that they were assigned at birth (typically their sex). So if you were assigned as a man at birth, and you still identify as a man, then you are cis.

Cisnormativity

The belief that being cis/cisgender is the normative gender identity to hold.

Gender dysphoria

Feeling uneasy and distressed about your relationship with your gender identity.

Heteronormativity

The belief that heterosexual attraction and relationships are the norm.

Inclusion

The act and practice of including people. Inclusion work usually focuses on those who have been excluded for unjustified reasons.

Intersectionality

A theory that describes how different parts of our identity provide us with certain advantages and disadvantages when in certain environments. These can combine, overlap, and intersect to produce unique experiences and obstacles for everybody. For example Black women are not only vulnerable to racism and misogyny, but can face specific disadvantageous experiences that are unique to Black women.

Justice

A state of fairness. Justice typically describes moral and lawful correctness.

LGBT/LGBTQIA+

These are acronyms that stand for lesbian, gay, bisexual, transgender (LGBT) and lesbian, gay, bisexual, transgender, Queer/questioning, Intersex and Asexual, respectively. The + is used to include other non-cis/heterosexual identities that aren't included in the acronym.

Marginalised

To be pushed to the edges of society and placed at a disadvantage. Marginalised groups are not always minority groups, yet often are.

Microaggression

A subtle, indirect and sometimes unintentional form of discrimination.

Misgendering

Referring to or describing someone in a way that doesn't align with their gender.

Non-binary

Someone whose gender identity is neither a man nor a woman.

Oppression

When a dominant group uses its power to systematically discriminate against and exploit a marginalised group.

People of Colour (POC)

A respectful way to describe people who are not White.

Patriarchy

An oppressive societal system that benefits cis men at the expense of all other genders.

Power

The ability to control others and manipulate situations to achieve your goals.

Prejudice

Holding a negative opinion about someone or something, typically without justified reason.

Privilege

Advantages you gain from an imbalance of power, that afford you unearned benefits. For example, White privilege.

Representation/Underrepresentation

The extent to which members of a certain demographic group are present within a certain environment or context. Underrepresentation is usually when a certain group is not adequately represented.

Society

A group of people who share common cultures, institutions, systems, values and interests. Society in the context of this book refers specifically to twenty-first century Western society.

Stereotype

To place generalised assumptions on a certain group, based on an oversimplified understanding and perception of them. This is harmful as it strips people of the right to individuality and can encourage prejudices.

Systemic

Relating to a system, which is a complex sum of interconnecting parts that are working towards common objectives.

Trans/Transgender

Someone whose gender identity is different from the one they were assigned at birth.

Voice

The extent to which you are able to be heard and have your opinions valued. Marginalised groups are typically lacking in voice.

Queer

A label used to describe a community of people that reject heteronormativity, which is the belief that being heterosexual and cisgender, and having cis/het sexual relationships is the norm. It can be used to describe people who are not cis or heterosexual. However, due to its history of being an oppressive slur, not all members of the LGBTQIA+ community agree with being described as Queer. Therefore don't assume that someone is comfortable with being described as Queer without confirmation.

White saviourism

Used to describe behaviour displayed by White people which indicates that think they have a superior ability to solve the problems faced by People of Colour.

REFERENCES

Bhatia, N. and Bhatia, S., 2020. Changes in Gender Stereotypes Over Time: A Computational Analysis. *Psychology of Women Quarterly*, [online] 45(1), pp.106-125. Available at: <https://journals.sagepub.com/doi/10.1177/0361684320977178>.

Bleiweis, R., 2020. *Quick Facts About the Gender Wage Gap*. [online] Center for American Progress. Available at <https://www.americanprogress.org/article/quick-facts-gender-wage-gap/> [Accessed 12 October 2022].

British Medical Association, 2021. *"A missed opportunity" - BMA response to the Race Report*. British Medical Association.

CDP UK, 2017. *CDP Carbon Majors Report 2017*. [online] CDP UK. Available at: <https://cdn.cdp.net/cdp-production/cms/reports/documents/000/002/327/original/Carbon-Majors-Report-2017.pdf?1501833772> [Accessed 12 October 2022].

Charities Aid Foundation (CAF), 2021. *Charities Aid Foundation UK Giving Report 2021*. [online] Charities Aid Foundation (CAF). Available at: <https://www.cafonline.org/docs/default-source/about-us-research/uk_giving_report_2021.pdf> [Accessed 12 October 2022].

Chartered Institute of Personnel and Development (CIPD), 2021. *Inclusion at Work: Perspectives on LGBT+ working lives*. [online] Chartered Institute of Personnel and Development (CIPD). Available at: <https://www.cipd.co.uk/Images/inclusion-work-perspectives-report_tcm18-90359.pdf> [Accessed 12 October 2022].

Covey, R., S., 1989. *The seven habits of highly effective people*. New York: Simon and Schuster.

Crenshaw, K., 1989. Demarginalizing the Intersection of Race and Sex: A Black Feminist Critique of Antidiscrimination Doctrine, Feminist Theory and Antiracist Politics. *University of Chicago Legal Forum*, 1989(1).

Five Cities Tackling Air Pollution (2022) UNEP. Available at: https://www.unep.org/news-and-stories/story/five-cities-tackling-air-pollution#:~:text=Air%20pollution%20has%20been%20called,heart%20disease%20and%20lung%20cancer. (Accessed: November 7, 2022).

Forti, V., Baldé, P., C., Kuehr, R. and Bel, G., 2020. *The Global E-waste Monitor 2020: Quantities, flows and the circular economy potential*. [online] Bonn/Geneva/Rotterdam: United Nations University (UNU)/United Nations Institute for

Training and Research (UNITAR) – co-hosted SCYCLE Programme, International Telecommunication Union (ITU) & International Solid Waste Association (ISWA). Available at: <https://www.itu.int/en/ITU-D/Environment/Documents/Toolbox/GEM_2020_def.pdf> [Accessed 12 October 2022

Freedman, G., Burgoon, E., Ferrell, J., Pennebaker, J. and Beer, J., 2017. When Saying Sorry May Not Help: The Impact of Apologies on Social Rejections. *Frontiers in Psychology*, [online] 8. Available at: <https://www.frontiersin.org/articles/10.3389/fpsyg.2017.01375/full>.

Frimer, A., J., Skitka, J., L. and Motyl, M., 2017. Liberals and conservatives are similarly motivated to avoid exposure to one another's opinions. *Journal of Experimental Social Psychology*, [online] 72, pp.1-12. Available at: <https://www.sciencedirect.com/science/article/pii/S0022103116304024> [Accessed 12 October 2022].

Gilead, M., Sela, M. and Maril, A., 2018. That's My Truth: Evidence for Involuntary Opinion Confirmation. *Social Psychological and Personality Science*, [online] 10(3), pp.393-401. Available at: <https://journals.sagepub.com/doi/abs/10.1177/1948550618762300>.

Glynn, T., Gamarel, K., Kahler, C., Iwamoto, M., Operario, D. and Nemoto, T., 2016. The role of gender affirmation in psychological well-being among transgender women. *Psychology of Sexual Orientation and Gender Diversity*, [online] 3(3), pp.336-344. Available at: <https://www.ncbi.nlm.nih.gov/pmc/articles/PMC5061456/>.

265

GOV.UK. 2020. *Police powers and procedures, England and Wales, year ending 31 March 2020 second edition.* [online] Available at: <https://www.gov.uk/government/statistics/police-powers-and-procedures-england-and-wales-year-ending-31-march-2020> [Accessed 12 October 2022].

Greenpeace & Everyday Plastic, 2022. *The Big Plastic Count Results.* [online] Greenpeace & Everyday Plastic. Available at: <https://thebigplasticcount.com/media/The-Big-Plastic-Count-Results-Report.pdf> [Accessed 12 October 2022].

Interaction Institute for Social Change, 2016. *Illustrating Equality VS Equity.* [image] Available at: <https://interactioninstitute.org/illustrating-equality-vs-equity/> [Accessed 12 October 2022].

Kramer, A., Guillory, J. and Hancock, J., 2014. Experimental evidence of massive-scale emotional contagion through social networks. *Proceedings of the National Academy of Sciences,* [online] 111(24), pp.8788-8790. Available at: <https://www.pnas.org/doi/10.1073/pnas.1320040111>.

Lee, K., Esposito, G. and Setoh, P., 2018. Preschoolers Favor Their Ingroup When Resources Are Limited. *Frontiers in Psychology,* [online] 9. Available at: <https://www.frontiersin.org/articles/10.3389/fpsyg.2018.01752/full>.

Lorde, A., 1988. *A Burst of Light: and Other Essays.* New York: Firebrand Books.

McKinsey & Company and LeanIn.Org, 2021. *Women in the Workplace 2021*. [online] McKinsey & Company. Available at: <https://wiw-report.s3.amazonaws.com/Women_in_the_Workplace_2021.pdf> [Accessed 12 October 2022].

Morelli, S., Ong, D., Makati, R., Jackson, M. and Zaki, J., 2017. Empathy and well-being correlate with centrality in different social networks. *Proceedings of the National Academy of Sciences*, [online] 114(37), pp.9843-9847. Available at: <https://www.pnas.org/doi/full/10.1073/pnas.1702155114>.

Nadal, K., 2018. *Microaggressions and traumatic stress*. Washington, DC: American Psychological Association.

Ons.gov.uk. 2021. *Gender pay gap in the UK - Office for National Statistics*. [online] Available at: <https://www.ons.gov.uk/employmentandlabourmarket/peopleinwork/earningsandworkinghours/bulletins/genderpaygapintheuk/2021> [Accessed 12 October 2022].

Oprah.com. 2010. *Oprah Talks to Thich Nhat Hanh*. [online] Available at: <https://www.oprah.com/spirit/oprah-talks-to-thich-nhat-hanh/all> [Accessed 12 October 2022].

Our World in Data. 2018. *Global inequalities in CO emissions*. [online] Available at: <https://ourworldindata.org/co2-by-income-region> [Accessed 12 October 2022].

Park, J., Vani, P., Saint-Hilaire, S. and Kraus, M., 2022. Disadvantaged group activists' attitudes toward advantaged group allies in social movements. *Journal of Experimental Social Psychology*, [online] 98, p.104226. Available at: <https://www.sciencedirect.com/science/article/pii/S0022103121001293>.

Pew Research Center: Internet, Science & Tech. 2021. *The State of Online Harassment*. [online] Available at: <https://www.pewresearch.org/internet/2021/01/13/the-state-of-online-harassment/> [Accessed 12 October 2022].

Plan International, 2018. *Unsafe in the city*. Plan International.

Queen Mary University of London & the University of York, 2020. *Accent Bias in Britain*. [online] Queen Mary University of London & the University of York. Available at: <https://accentbiasbritain.org/wp-content/uploads/2020/03/Accent-Bias-Britain-Report-2020.pdf> [Accessed 12 October 2022].

Sabin, J. and Greenwald, A., 2012. The Influence of Implicit Bias on Treatment Sabin, J. and Greenwald, A., 2012. The Influence of Implicit Bias on Treatment Recommendations for 4 Common Pediatric Conditions: Pain, Urinary Tract Infection, Attention Deficit Hyperactivity Disorder, and Asthma. *American Journal of Public Health*, [online] 102(5), pp.988-995. Available at: <https://pubmed.ncbi.nlm.nih.gov/22420817/>.

Sears, B.S. et al. (2021) LGBT PEOPLE'S EXPERIENCES OF WORKPLACE DISCRIMINATION AND HARASSMENT. rep. Available at: https://williamsinstitute.law.ucla.edu/

wp-content/uploads/Workplace-Discrimination-Sep-2021.
pdf (Accessed: November 7, 2022).

Schwartz, B., 2016. *The paradox of choice*. New York: Ecco.

Snopes.com. 2005. *Were Hurricane Katrina 'Looting'
Photographs Captioned Differently Based on Race?*. [online]
Available at: <https://www.snopes.com/fact-check/
hurricane-katrina-looters/> [Accessed 12 October 2022].

Social Metrics Commission, 2019. *Measuring Poverty 2019
– The Social Metrics Commission*. [online] The Legatum
Institute. Available at: <https://socialmetricscommission.
org.uk/wp-content/uploads/2019/07/SMC_measuring-
poverty-201908_full-report.pdf> [Accessed 12 October
2022].

Stern, G., 2019. Altruism: Giving for Mental Well-Being.
Journal of the American Psychiatric Nurses Association, 25(4),
pp.314-315.

Surgo Ventures, 2021. *Why do so many suffer silently with
mental health difficulties instead of seeking care?*. [online]
Surgo Ventures. Available at: <https://mentalhealth.
surgoventures.org/uk> [Accessed 12 October 2022].

Sutton Trust & Social Mobility Commission, 2019. *Elitist
Britain 2019*. [online] Sutton Trust & Social Mobility
Commission. Available at: <https://assets.publishing.service.
gov.uk/government/uploads/system/uploads/attachment_
data/file/811045/Elitist_Britain_2019.pdf> [Accessed 12
October 2022].

Tabassum, N. and Nayak, B., 2021. Gender Stereotypes and Their Impact on Women's Career Progressions from a Managerial Perspective. *IIM Kozhikode Society & Management Review*, [online] 10(2), pp.192-208. Available at: <https://journals.sagepub.com/doi/full/10.1177/2277975220975513>.

TED, 2010. The power of vulnerability. [video] Available at: <https://www.ted.com/talks/brene_brown_the_power_of_vulnerability?language=en> [Accessed 12 October 2022].

The GEMM project, 2019. *Are employers in Britain discriminating against ethnic minorities?*. [online] The GEMM project. Available at: <http://csi.nuff.ox.ac.uk/wp-content/uploads/2019/01/Are-employers-in-Britain-discriminating-against-ethnic-minorities_final.pdf> [Accessed 12 October 2022].

The International Society of Aesthetic Plastic Surgery (ISAPS), 2022. *Latest Global Survey from ISAPS Reports Continuing Rise in Aesthetic Surgery Worldwide*. [online] The International Society of Aesthetic Plastic Surgery (ISAPS). Available at: <https://www.isaps.org/wp-content/uploads/2020/12/ISAPS-Global-Survey-2019-Press-Release-English.pdf> [Accessed 12 October 2022].

The Trevor Project, 2020. *The Trevor Project's 2020 National Survey on LGBTQ Youth Mental Health*. [online] The Trevor Project. Available at: <https://www.thetrevorproject.org/wp-content/uploads/2020/07/The-Trevor-Project-National-Survey-Results-2020.pdf> [Accessed 12 October 2022].

Tomm, B. and Zhao, J., 2017. Resource scarcity impairs visual online detection and prospective memory. *Journal of Vision*, [online] 17(10), p.99. Available at: <https://zhaolab.psych.ubc.ca/pdfs/Tomm_Zhao_2017_CogSci.pdf>.

Transport for London. 2021. *TfL asks customers to help shape the future of step-free access.* [online] Available at: <https://tfl.gov.uk/info-for/media/press-releases/2021/november/tfl-asks-customers-to-help-shape-the-future-of-step-free-access#:~:text=Over%20half%20(51%25)%20of,and%20the%20Northern%20Line%20Extension> [Accessed 12 October 2022].

UNHCR – Climate Change and disaster displacement (2021) UNHCR. Available at: https://www.unhcr.org/climate-change-and-disasters.html (Accessed: November 7, 2022).

U.S. Environmental Protection Agency, EPA, 2021. *Climate Change and Social Vulnerability in the United States: A Focus on Six Impacts.* [online] U.S. Environmental Protection Agency, EPA. Available at: <https://www.epa.gov/system/files/documents/2021-09/climate-vulnerability_september-2021_508.pdf> [Accessed 12 October 2022].

Vox. 2020. *The systemic racism black Americans face, explained in 9 charts.* [online] Available at: <https://www.vox.com/2020/6/17/21284527/systemic-racism-black-americans-9-charts-explained> [Accessed 12 October 2022].

Wilson, J., Hugenberg, K. and Rule, N., 2017. Racial bias in judgments of physical size and formidability: From size to threat. *Journal of Personality and Social Psychology*, [online] 113(1), pp.59-80. Available at: <https://www.apa.org/pubs/journals/releases/psp-pspi0000092.pdf>.

Yale University and George Mason University, 2019. *Climate Change in the American Mind*. New Haven, CT: Yale Program on Climate Change Communication.

YouGov & Stonewall, 2018. *LGBT in Britain - Work Report*. Stonewall.

Yougov.co.uk. 2015. *Oh, sorry: Do British people really apologise too much? | YouGov*. [online] Available at: <https://yougov.co.uk/topics/lifestyle/articles-reports/2015/07/01/oh-sorry-do-british-people-apologise-too-much> [Accessed 12 October 2022].

Zhao, K., Ferguson, E. and Smillie, L., 2017. Politeness and Compassion Differentially Predict Adherence to Fairness Norms and Interventions to Norm Violations in Economic Games. *Scientific Reports*, [online] 7(1), pp.1-11. Available at: <https://www.nature.com/articles/s41598-017-02952-1.pdf>.